1972

Preparing Your Child for Reading

Preparing Your Child for Reading
by Miles A. Tinker

Holt, Rinehart and Winston
New York, Chicago, San Francisco

To
Katherine Howland Tinker

Contents

Preface

This book is written to help parents prepare their child for reading. Most parents hope their child will learn to read successfully during the first grade of school. The material in this book is designed to aid the parent in providing preschool experiences that are basic to learning to read. Also considered are up-to-date programs in the kindergarten and the possibility for some children of beginning reading before entering first grade. Although the book is primarily for parents, it will also be helpful to teachers in kindergarten and the primary grades. The advice to parents and teachers is based upon sound practice and research.

Emphasis is placed upon maintaining a good relationship between the parents and their child. Informal evaluation of the child's capabilities is presented as an aid to the parents in selecting experiences for him that are in accordance with successive levels of his development. This will help the parents to guard against expecting too much or too little of their child. Experiences readily available in and outside the home that will help to prepare the child for reading are described. Special emphasis is placed upon the development of verbal facility which is of prime importance in learning to read. Ways in which the parent can foster visual and auditory discrimination are described. These skills are of high value in learning to read. Healthy growth in both physical and mental abilities, dependent to a considerable extent upon parental care, is also essential. How picture books and reading to the child can be used advantageously to prepare him for reading is discussed. The program in the kindergarten that will best prepare the child for reading is explained in some detail. After the child enters school, emphasis is placed upon coordinated relationship between the parents, the teacher, and the child. Lists of books suitable for reading to the child and for him to read are given in Appendix A. Most of these books can be borrowed from a public library.

School systems, publishers, and individuals have contributed directly or indirectly to this volume. To them I give grateful acknowledgment. Special help was obtained from: *Handbook for Parents* and *Pre-Primary Guide and Supplement* organized by the preprimary teachers in the Evansville-Vanderburgh School Corporation, Evansville, Indiana, 1966; Marion Monroe and Bernice Rogers, *Foundations for Reading*, Scott, Foresman and Company, Chicago, 1964; Paul McKee, Joseph E. Brzeinski, and M. Lucile Harrison, *The Effectiveness of Teaching Reading in Kindergarten*, The Denver Public Schools and The Colorado State Department of Education, Denver, Colorado, 1966; and James L. Hymes, Jr., *Before the Child Reads*, Row, Peterson and Company, Evanston, Illinois, 1958.

I am especially indebted to Mrs. Robin Kyriakis for her extensive, careful, and helpful editorial suggestions.

M. A. T.

Santa Barbara, California
February 1971

Chapter 1.
The Parent-Child Relationship

The parents are the first teachers of their child and throughout childhood and adolescence are likely to be the most important teachers he will ever have. Every parent wants his child to feel secure and happy and to grow and develop normally. The parent hopes that by the time his child enters first grade he will be ready and eager to learn to read and that he will get along well with the other children and with his teacher.

Most parents are not aware of how much they themselves can do to realize this hope. Many of the materials and situations they will need for teaching the preschool child are already available in the home and neighborhood. But materials and learning situations and knowing how to use them are not enough. Basic to all learning is the relationship between teacher and learner. Mutual trust and confidence, shared enthusiasms, and ease of communication are essential. That is why this first chapter is devoted to the parent-child relationship.

(The use of the pronouns *he, his,* and *him,* throughout this book follows an established rule to use these pronouns when the meanings *he* and/or *she* and *his, him,* and/or *her* are implied. This book, of course, concerns both girls and boys.)

The child is fortunate who has two parents to guide him during his formative years. Each parent makes a unique contribution to the child's development. However, to some extent the parental roles can be interchanged, depending upon circumstance and personalities. When the mother must be employed outside the home, the father may very well take over some of her traditional functions, such as giving baths and putting the children to bed. In some families it is the father who most enjoys taking the children on hikes and teaching them to swim, but it may be the mother who prefers to do this and the father who is at his best in play activities around the home.

It is also recognized that in many families parts of the parental role must be delegated to others. The child may spend weekdays with his grandmother or some other adult while his mother is employed, or the father's work may take him away from home for days or weeks at a time. There may or may not be an older brother, grandfather, or uncle for the child to turn to during these absences of his father. In such family situations, it is all the more important for both parents to be as well versed as possible in what their child needs to develop properly so that together they can maintain the parent-child relationship on a high level in spite of obstacles. Such understanding will also help them to choose wisely and to note carefully the results when it is necessary to place their child with others for a considerable period of time. It has been said that it is not how much time the parent spends with his child but how he spends it. There is some truth in this statement. But that does not affect the importance of choosing a suitable person to supervise the child when the parent is away.

By the time the child reaches two years of age, his father as well as his mother is at the center of his small world. While he loves to receive their approval, he is also needing to assert himself as a person in his own right, and sometimes it may seem that *no* is the only word he knows. Some parents then feel that their good baby has rather suddenly become a naughty child. This, of course, is not true, however frustrating to the parents his negative behavior may at times become. Some of their frustration stems from the narrow limits of verbal communication with such a young child. This is a period when actions definitely speak louder to him than words and are better understood. But tone of voice and smiles or frowns convey meaning to the child and he also understands many more words than he can speak.

So, respect his need to set himself apart by saying "no" or doing the opposite from what he knows is expected of him, and strive for a proper balance between permissiveness and restraint. He expects you to keep him safe, that is, to see that he does not harm himself or others, or get into trouble by destroying things. He takes it for granted that you will protect him. When he says "no," punishment is not in order for he is merely trying to be himself. Instead, you might reply, "All right. Let's wait a little while." If he is saying "no" to getting ready for bed, you could pick up a picture book he likes and say, "Well, I'm going into the bedroom, so come soon." If left alone, he will probably soon follow you, feeling that he is doing so quite on his own. Supposing the two-year-old scribbles with his crayons on the living room wall. It will probably be enough to show regret by saying sadly, "That's too bad. Just look at the wall! How can we get it off?" Then, give him paper and tell him that paper is for crayons, and he can mark it all he wants to. He may not understand all the words you use, but he learns how to win your approval, which is what he wants to do. You did not grab the crayon away from him or blame him by scolding, and so you avoided provoking a negative response. And you redirected his energies into safe channels.

This type of problem may seem far removed from that of preparing your child for reading, but is it really? The child who has learned to be afraid of expressing himself and who expects criticism and punishment whenever he does something not pleasing to adults will be slow to develop self-respect and trust in others. When beginning reading, he may very well be afraid to make mistakes or even attempt something so difficult while under the watchful eye of a teacher whom he does not yet know or trust. What goes on between parent and child is the child's introduction to all human relationships. A parent who is overprotective or indifferent or repressive toward his child sets up barriers which may stand in his way for years to come when he tries to relate to other people at school and elsewhere. Only when the child feels loved and secure does he feel that he is somebody, dares to explore his world, has ideas of his own and tests them out, and turns confidently to those around him for answers to his questions. He then develops confidence that he can learn to do whatever grown-ups do, such as read books and write stories.

With the slightly older child who can put at least some of his thoughts and feelings into words, the parent encounters somewhat different problems. The child may "talk back," stubbornly remain silent, or pleasantly evade an issue as though he did not get the point. While any of these reactions are to be expected occasionally, they often reflect some lack of understanding or sympathy on the part of the parent. The art of communicating with a child comes more easily to some adults than to others, but, while practice will not make perfect, it will always be helpful if undertaken with positive attitudes. First of all, the grown-up must learn to be a very good listener, to be genuinely interested in what the child knows, thinks, imagines, feels, and is curious about. Then he must learn not to be unnecessarily restrictive or judgmental. This is often especially difficult with your own child, for you tend to be overanxious about his behavior and overeager to have him think and feel as you do, or in what you regard as acceptable ways.

When your four-year-old says, "I hate you," you may be disturbed, forgetting that there have been moments when you felt no great love for him. But you have learned to handle many of your angry and negative feelings, so now you can be his teacher. Cheerfully tell him that you are glad he can tell you how he feels, that sometimes you feel angry, too. Point out that feelings are real and sometimes hard to understand, but it is quite all right to have them and to share them with you. Then you can go on to talk over with him whatever has been troubling him. Later he will learn when and where it may not be wise to voice all his feelings.

As your child develops from two to three years of age and on to four and five, he will pose many questions for you to answer. Try to tell him whatever he wants to know. If you turn him away too often, however good the reason seems at the time, he may cease to come to you with his questions. To stifle curiosity by not answering questions is to start closing the door on an inquiring mind. If you cannot answer some of his questions, do the best you can at the moment and then take the time to look up further information. Take the child with you when you consult the dictionary or some other book of reference. You will not only find the answer to his questions but many other facts that will interest him.

There are two kinds of approval of a child's behavior: general and specific. It is usually better to be specific. Praise should relate to the child's efforts and his competence and skill in doing things rather than to his disposition and mood and the kind of person he is. For instance, when he has helped with the dusting, it is appropriate to make a favorable comment on his work and to notice how clean and shiny the table and chairs now look. This is better than talking about what a good child he was to help you. Praise of effort and of work done is the best way to give approval. Your child can then draw his own inferences about what a good child he is, while taking pride in his actual accomplishments.

Bedtime is a very special part of the day to the young child. It should be a happy time. He needs a pleasant ending to the day's activities, such as a bedtime story and a feeling of closeness to the parent who puts him to bed. It is a good time to get to know your child better and to invite confidences through unhurried conversation that may not have been possible during the day. When relaxed and feeling secure and happy, your child is ready for sleep.

If there is more than one child in the family, the parents need not be surprised if some jealousy appears, particularly in an older child toward the new baby. Even careful inclusion of the older child in planning for the baby may not keep him from becoming jealous, although it does usually help. Both the only child who has had the undivided attention of his parents and the child who has often felt ignored will have difficulty in accepting the presence of a new baby. Here again, encouraging the child to express his rivalrous feelings without fear of criticism is a first step. Depending upon this expression, appropriate steps may need to be taken to guard against his harming the baby, both for the baby's sake and his own. In any case, the child should be verbally assured that he is loved just as always. In addition, the parents, especially the mother, should find ways to demonstrate this love. They can do this by giving him special honor and attention and by providing new interests and safe outlets for his negative feelings. Hostile feelings can often be reduced by acting them out. Depending upon the age and preferences of the child, a new dart board, a ball to bounce from the garage door, some old dolls with which he can do whatever he likes, even dismember them, may suit his mood. Also, the mother should manage to find a little time each day to spend with the older child while the baby is sleeping, or is in another room. The father can help, too, by undertaking some special activity with his preschool son or daughter, such as playing a new or favorite game each night, going fishing, or repainting the doll house. Gradually, as he becomes ready for it, the older child can be called upon to share with his mother in the baby's care and encouraged to take pride in being the older sibling.

When there are several children in the family, the parents have an excellent opportunity to help the pre-school child learn to play and work with brothers and sisters of various ages. There will be some rivalries and quarrels. As long as the young child is not being unduly threatened or endangered in any way, the parents will do well to stay in the background. This is often hard for the parents to do, but becomes easier when they remember that it will not be long before he will be pretty much on his own in the playground and elsewhere. He should be learning as fast as he can how to handle himself with other children whether they are always friendly and con-siderate or not. Older brothers and sisters can be taken aside on occasion and reminded to make proper allowance for the younger child's smaller size, lesser skill and experi-ence. If they are already well aware of the standards of behavior set within the family, an occasional reminder may be sufficient. Also, just knowing that a parent is nearby will help them to control and properly direct their actions. A parent or other competent older person should be readily available when the young child encounters serious problems of interaction with other children. Un-less the situation itself can be promptly straightened out, it is advisable to remove the child from it. Of course this should be done as tactfully as possible.

Conversing with your child is an important part of his education. As you talk with him about his interests, what you are doing, and what is going on around him, you will be helping to increase his vocabulary, improve his speech patterns, and stimulate his thought, thus preparing him for reading. Also, in such conversation, the parent can become better acquainted with his child, the way he feels and thinks, what he wonders about and imagines, what troubles him, and what he finds enjoyable and exciting. As we shall note throughout this book, verbal ability is one of the most valuable assets in learning to read. Only by conversation is your child likely to learn to express himself freely and well.

In developing a good relationship with your child, it is helpful to know something about what behavior can be reasonably expected at the different age levels. It must always be kept in mind that no two children reach a given level in exactly the same length of time and in the same way. One child may be precocious in motor development and slow in speech while another may be just the opposite. When we speak in generalities, these differences may not be apparent. Only identical twins tend to be alike. Otherwise, there are differences in general ability, personality traits, social aptitudes, motor ability, and other traits. (See Chapters 2 and 9.) Parents need to watch for, and take account of, the unique abilities and character traits of each child. Discussions in the following chapters will include more about this.

What is the usual behavior of the two-year-old? He is no longer an infant, but he is still immature compared with the three-year-old. The two-year-old goes through a period of rapid development during which the child becomes more and more aware of himself as an individual. Motor activity markedly increases, and his attention span is short. As he is only beginning to learn what is permissible and what is not, and has not learned to control his behavior accordingly, he needs close supervision. Left to his own devices, he may explore bureau drawers and bottles under the sink or pull books off the shelf. He has little or no idea of what he should or should not do and is naturally frustrated when pleasurable activity is interrupted. Also, he is finding that he can resist and say "no."

On the other hand, he now enjoys many acceptable activities. He is becoming much more interested in toys, preferring those that move, make noises, or can be pushed or pulled about. He likes to play with blocks or with a pan or small pail that can be filled with sand, pebbles, or water and then dumped. Usually he does not stay long with one activity but will return to it again and again. He likes to share in whatever his mother is doing, such as setting the table, making the beds, and cleaning the bathroom. Clothes are beginning to interest him, and he may like one outfit much better than another. He needs much help in dressing but is delighted whenever he is able to do part of it himself, such as finding and putting on his shoes, even though he cannot fasten them. The feeling of ownership is growing: his clothes and his toys are already definitely his, and usually he will not share them. He may also be very possessive about little things he collects, such as pebbles, sticks, or bits of crayon. His vocabulary is increasing, and he understands many more words than he uses. Often the two-year-old has a definite preference for his mother or his father, although this may alternate according to the time of day or the type of activity.

The fourth year is a busy, happy period, a time of early childhood's coming of age. The three-year-old is becoming more self-reliant and has more self-control. He is usually cooperative, accepting suggestions cheerfully. His mother will find him of considerable help in running simple errands, finding things, or putting things away. Her directions are understood, and he can now ask when he has forgotten them or does not know what to do next. Feeding himself is less of a problem, and he can dress himself with less help. His command of language is increasing in range and depth, and he likes to experiment with new words. Picture books, stories, and songs now hold his attention more readily. (See Chapter 7.) He enjoys using crayons in a coloring book. His new skills and growing independence enable him to spend more time playing by himself, but he is not yet ready to play for extended periods with others of his age unless under competent supervision. Care must be taken not to expect too much of the three-year-old who sometimes seems so mature but who, when tired or otherwise out of sorts, can revert so quickly to more babyish behavior.

Around four years of age, the child becomes more assertive and less content with the simple enjoyments of the three-year-old. He has more ideas, makes more demands, and is less amenable to suggestions. In contrast with younger children, he now talks while eating. In fact, he has become a great talker, likes new words, and asks lots of questions. In practicing with words, he tends to exaggerate, enjoy silly repetitions, make little jokes, and bring forth some very fanciful ideas. He is trying to grow up—to be like a five-year-old. Also, he loves to dress up and pretend he is an adult.

The four-year-old is developing a strong identity with home which still means more to him than the less familiar outside. He tends to boast to outsiders and to quote his mother and father as authorities. Playing with one other child of about his own age now is usually successful, but he may not adjust well to more than one playmate at a time without supervision. But when an adult is close by to anticipate and prevent unnecessary clashes by seeing that all are engaging in some enjoyable activity, the four-year-old will benefit from becoming accustomed to group play. Although he will now share some of his toys more willingly than when younger, he tends to demand his own way and is not yet accustomed to taking turns.

Books are becoming of greater interest, and he will

examine pictures in more detail and talk about them. The four-year-old likes repetition of familiar stories, parts of which he now knows by heart, and new stories that are informative, humorous, or full of action. He also likes nonsense rhymes and poetry with vivid imagery and strong rhythms. Many four-year-olds already know a few songs, will try to join in on less familiar ones, and enjoy simple singing and marching games. His increasing curiosity about the "why" of everything now makes worthwhile little excursions to places in line with his interests. See Chapter 5 for a discussion of experiences outside the home.

At five years, the child is beginning to be clear, concise, and complete in his language behavior. He can now dress himself satisfactorily and does not need so much help in washing, combing his hair, or the like. And he can really help with simple household tasks, such as setting the table, bringing in the milk bottles, collecting the wastebaskets for emptying, and making his bed. He knows where his toys belong and with encouragement will put them away. He does such tasks more efficiently and with less dawdling.

With improved motor control and increased ability to observe and to note details, he makes better drawings and tends to choose the right colors for familiar objects pictured in his coloring book. Most children at this age are not yet ready for reading. (See Chapter 12.) Even though your child may be in kindergarten at age five, he still needs continued guidance at home in preparation for reading. (See Chapter 11.) And he is now ready for wider experiences in the community. (Again, see Chapter 5.) Although he still enjoys flights of imagination, he welcomes more encounters with reality.

The above discussion merely outlines some of the usual behavior traits of children at the various preschool ages.

The alert parent who spends time with his child will make many more pertinent observations which will help in meeting his child's needs as they develop.

If the parent and child have developed a sound, comfortable relationship, full of love and mutual respect, the child will be ready to set forth confidently on his first day of school. He will expect to like his teacher and the other children, and he will be ready and able to apply himself to the major undertaking of the first grade—learning to read.

Chapter 2.
Looking Ahead to Reading

To understand and appreciate what preparation your child needs for learning to read, let us consider what the child has to do to get the meaning from written or printed language. First, we must appreciate that reading is talk written down. That is, learning to read involves learning that printed symbols stand for speech. Your child reads when he not only says the right printed words but also understands their meaning because of his prior experience in comprehending the words spoken in meaningful sequence. He soon finds that printed words "talk" sense. Quite early, the child discovers that finding meanings is the core of the reading process. As he advances in school, he acquires skill in word recognition, in proceeding from left to right along a line of print, and in recognizing the relation of single words to phrases and sentences. He increases his vocabulary and the range and depth of his ideas. He learns that reading is thinking, and he acquires the knack of reading by thought units. In silent reading he no longer has to vocalize or even move his lips.

Reading is a complex process. Even so, as the child progresses in reading, his word-recognition methods operate with ease and speed. The material read becomes more complicated as to vocabulary, ideas, length and structure of sentences, and complexity of language. The role of thinking while reading increases in importance. To become a good reader, your child must learn to interpret, evaluate, and reflect upon the meanings encountered. Therefore, mere recognition of words is not enough. The thinking side of reading must be developed, or the process of learning from the printed page will remain relatively ineffective. To be a mature reader, the child must also become a critical reader.

Progress from left to right along a line of print does not come naturally but must be learned. The order of the words must be pointed out to the child many times. Then, he will learn how to progress from left to right in viewing a series of pictures that tell a story. When he starts to read, considerable practice and guidance will still be necessary on how to move in the proper direction in reading words in a line of print. Preparatory exercises for the preschool child are given in Chapter 8.

Development of a large speaking vocabulary forms the basis for perceiving printed words. An ever-increasing vocabulary "bank" of meaningful words is constantly drawn upon by the good reader in order to understand the meanings of words and phrases encountered in his reading. Meanings come from previous experience, including usage of the words in communication with others. This experience needs to be wide and varied. Without a clear understanding of words, the meanings of sentences and paragraphs cannot be grasped.

Comprehension of sentences is not easy. Besides an understanding of word meanings, several other skills are needed. One of these skills is the ability to grasp the relations between words and groups of words. The reader must learn to read by phrases or thought units. Other necessary skills include interpretation of punctuation and ability to comprehend figures of speech and symbolic expressions. Understanding the relation between several parts of a sentence is called "sentence sense." Sentence structure is sometimes complex. For instance, the subject may come last or between two parts of the predicate rather than at the beginning. Another difficulty in understanding some sentences is that of identifying the thing or person referred to by a pronoun. To comprehend larger units, such as a paragraph, the reader needs to understand the relation between sentences. This includes identifying the topic sentence which will give the key to the central thought in the paragraph and how it is related to the amplifying sentences.

In word recognition the child needs to recognize the initial letter, middle letters, and the final letter or letters. This requires rather fine discrimination of letter forms and sounds. Letters such as *b, p,* and *d* often give children difficulty. Sounds may be even more difficult because so many letters have more than one sound. Besides knowing the sounds of the letters, the reader must learn how to blend letter sounds into a word. This is not easy for some children. A child may know the sounds of all the letters in a word but be unable to blend them without considerable guidance and practice. See Chapter 7 for suggestions on teaching your child to listen to and to discriminate sounds.

Some parents who do not recall having had any difficulty themselves in learning to read are puzzled by the apparent frequency today of reading problems among both children and adults. It is true that a goodly number of children are mature enough upon entering first grade to learn to read without undue difficulty, even though their parents have not consciously tried to prepare them. But many others do badly in beginning reading if their readiness has been left to chance. The aim of our present-day program of education is to enable *all* children to learn up to their capacity. It is now recognized that many "dropouts" are practically nonreaders and that, under more favorable circumstances at home and at school, most of them could have learned to read and then might have continued happily and profitably in school. School can become intolerable to the child who becomes seriously backward in reading.

With adequate preparation, most children will acquire enough reading readiness to begin reading when they enter the first grade or soon afterward. A few are already reading when they enter school. When a child is truly ready to learn how to read, he can do so easily and efficiently. The essential requirements have been met, and he is able to make good use of reading instruction. If a child is not ready by the time he enters grade one, it is not wise for the teacher to put pressure on him to start beginning reading. Such forcing is apt to develop in the child a dislike for reading which may interfere for years to come with his educational development. Instead, the teacher should enlist the parent's cooperation in promoting greater reading readiness by increasing and enriching his experiences at home and at school. It is definitely better to prepare the child for reading before reading instruction is begun.

Reading readiness is not something that can be forced on the child, however. While the child is developing mentally and physically, the wise parent guides him by providing experiences that he is ready for at each of the age levels prior to school. That is, the child learns from experiences that he welcomes and enjoys because he is ready for them. Instead of spending money on exercise books and time on paper-and-pencil-drills, the parent will do better to make creative use of common everyday activities in the home and elsewhere to encourage her child to develop motor skills, verbal facility, powers of observation, and other abilities which tend to develop reading readiness. To do this successfully, the parent will need to know what kinds of experience the child is ready for at a particular age. There is no sense in exposing a child to experiences suitable for a three-year-old when he is barely two, unless he is unusually precocious. And not all children at any given age have reached the same level of ability in all respects. The parents must study their child as he develops in order to evaluate his capabilities. Chapter 3 describes how you can guide him into activities he is ready to enjoy and profit from at a particular time. The child should concentrate on what is good and significant and worthwhile in and of itself at the time. Succeeding chapters will present in more detail how you can evaluate your child's development and select experiences that are basic in preparing him for reading.

From the very beginning of reading instruction, comprehension is necessary. The child can understand what he is trying to read only if prior experience has provided him with an appropriate, meaningful vocabulary. Unless he can recognize familiar objects, situations, and actions in the pictures in his primer, that is "read" the pictures, he is not likely to know what the story is all about, even when it is told to him verbally. This means that he is not prepared to begin learning to read it. If you will examine a primer or two, you will find quite a range of subjects. There may be stories about putting up a tent, collecting eggs from a hen's nest, digging clams, a policeman directing traffic, building a snowman, driving a tractor, taking a trip on a jet plane, riding a camel, and many others. It is not necessary for the child to have experienced every one of these activities in order to "read" the pictures. But similar experiences are necessary. If he has had a pony ride or even watched riders on horseback, he can manage a picture story about camel riding. But if he has never been to a zoo or a farm and has no television, his first picture book about animals will put him at a real disadvantage.

Details of the development and experiences that the child needs in preparation for reading, now being outlined, will be discussed fully in the following chapters. After making an informal evaluation of your child's capabilities, you should examine which of the everyday experiences in the home are the most valuable in preparing your child for reading. These may include play activities, helping with household tasks, development of speech and vocabulary, acquiring independence in activities and thought, relating to other children and adults, and enjoying stories, songs, pictures, and books. In these various learning situations, keep in mind that you are the teacher, which is further discussed in Chapter 4.

Many experiences outside the home are also basic in preparing your child for reading. These include acquaintance with the neighborhood near his home, trips to stores when the parent is shopping, visiting a fire station, a park, a post office, a zoo, and other places when possible. Taking trips with parents to a farm, a lake or a river, or whatever places are new and interesting to the child will add to his knowledge and experience. This will be especially true when what he will see is explained to him and talked about in advance, as well as during the trip and after he returns home, as outlined in Chapter 5. He should feel free to ask questions and be confident that they will be taken seriously and answered to his satisfaction.

The child is continually adding new words to his vocabulary as he participates more and more in the activities of the home and as his experience outside the home is extended. Understanding the meaning of a new word does not necessarily result in its use. Encourage your child to try out new words in his conversation with you, appreciate his effort even when he makes mistakes, and guide him to correct usage. Include him in conversations with adults outside the family and make sure that he has frequent opportunity to talk with other children. Various ways to help your child develop verbal facility will be discussed in Chapter 6.

Reading also requires auditory skills. So it is necessary for your child to learn how to listen carefully and well. It is hard to imagine the world of strange sounds in which the young child finds himself. Adults easily recognize most of the sounds they hear, even without paying much attention, and they habitually disregard many of them. The child needs help in distinguishing between sounds so that by the time he reaches school he will have learned how to make many of the finer auditory discriminations required for reading. He will then hear differences in the various sounds of words and in their quality. Listening from an early age to stories told or read will give him good practice in learning speech sounds. For a few years in early childhood his attention span will be relatively short but in time, with practice and guidance, he will be able to listen attentively for longer and longer periods. Your child should be encouraged to think about what he hears and to ask questions. Auditory discrimination will be considered further in Chapter 7.

Training in seeing also serves to prepare the child for reading. Children begin at an early age to distinguish objects visually. This ability develops month by month and year by year. As the child grows older, he will be able to pay attention to smaller and smaller details and to discriminate between them. There is much that the parent can do to foster in the child the practice of making accurate visual observations which will prepare the way for distinguishing the many details on the printed page. Such training will of course continue after the child begins to learn to read. (See Chapter 8.)

Healthy development in both physical and mental abilities depends to a considerable degree upon parental care. Upon entering first grade, the child who is healthy, happy, and alert stands the best chance of adjusting well to the entire school situation. Learning to read depends on physical and emotional well-being. The child needs to be able to see clearly the printed symbols in books and what is written on the chalkboard. Hearing must be accurate, so that without undue effort the differences in verbal sounds can be discriminated correctly. And motor control of eyes, hands, and speech organs is necessary for moving the eyes properly along a line of writing or print, for eye-hand coordination in writing and drawing and turning the pages of a book, and for correct pronunciation of words. During the child's earlier years, a certain amount of awkwardness and clumsiness is to be expected. With skilled and sympathetic guidance on the part of parent and teacher, improvement in motor skills can be expected to occur gradually as a part of the growth process.

Defects in vision and hearing should be detected at an early age, well before the child enters school. This is not usually difficult for the observant and concerned parent. If there is any doubt about your child's having normal speech or hearing, you should seek a doctor's advice. Should a defect be discovered, it should be corrected or remedied before the child is old enough for school. If the difficulty cannot be entirely corrected, the child should be helped to adjust to it before the school years and the adjustment continued in cooperation with the school. This subject is discussed further in Chapter 9.

The child's interest in books should be awakened as early as two years of age. (A list of suitable books for children appears in Appendix A at the back of this book.)

At first, the book is just a new object to be handled, but the two-year-old will see something of interest to him in some of the pictures, and he can enjoy very short stories. As he progresses through the preschool years, he will find more and more to enjoy in picture books and will learn how to "read" pictures. The stories and verses read to him will gradually hold his attention for longer periods, and he will like to talk about them. Although you are not teaching your child to read, you are acquainting him with some of the pleasures to be derived from books and helping him to develop habits of listening to and talking about the stories in them. During the preschool period, every child will enjoy acquiring a few picture books of his own and can be taught to treasure and care for them. (See Chapter 10.)

Many children at five years of age will have the opportunity of attending kindergarten and at six years will be starting first grade. Even after this, parents continue to be teachers of their children, guiding them in widening their experience at home and elsewhere. When your child is attending school, and especially during the early grades, you should have frequent contact and a close working relationship with his teacher and the school. The parent can keep the teacher in touch with the child's growth and development outside of school and with any problems arising that may have a bearing on his school adjustment. Likewise, the teacher acquaints the parent with the child's progress in school and with any problems that may develop. Together they can work out what steps each may try to help the child do better at school and at home. The parent is not doing his part by just going to an occasional PTA meeting. There is additional discussion of this subject in Chapter 11.

Should your child learn to read while in kindergarten? It is true that a few children are reading even before they enter kindergarten, and others are ready to begin while they are there. But a formal program of teaching reading to all kindergarten children seems ill-advised. However, for the child who is already reading, provision should be made for him to continue. And children who are ready should be given the opportunity to begin to learn to read, to the extent permitted by the facilities in the kindergarten room and the time the teacher can make available. Many of the children in kindergarten will not be ready for reading instruction, and some will not even be ready when they enter first grade. For these children, appropriate experiences should be provided to complete their reading readiness. In addition to more practice in learning to listen, in following directions, in using and adding to their vocabulary, and so on, they can be taught to recognize some lettters of the alphabet, their printed name, certain traffic signs, and numbers from 1 to 10. Chapter 12 discusses this more fully.

Preparing your child for reading does not end after the first few weeks of starting to read in the first grade. As new and more advanced reading material is encountered, the child needs an ever-increasing background of experience so that his comprehension can keep pace with the subject matter. For example, the concepts of city and state will be shadowy at best for the child whose experience has been limited to small towns. Every child will also need guidance in acquiring and understanding such abstract concepts as honor and justice. Without the continuing active participation of the parents in guiding and enriching the life of the child at home, the school at best can only approximate what is needed to enable the child to progress through the grades. As a matter of fact, preparation for reading at more and more advanced levels should continue throughout the school years, as outlined in Chapter 13.

Parents who understand the nature of reading and the kind of preparation for reading their child needs will find that they can provide all, or at least a large portion, of the experience which will enable him to adapt readily to the reading situation. These experiences should start at an early age and continue up to the time he enters first grade, and even beyond. Certain aspects of preparing the child to read should be continued and further developed all through the grades as he encounters new subjects and more complex reading material.

Chapter 3.
Informal Evaluation of the Child's Capabilities

Guidance of your child in experiences that will prepare him for reading depends upon knowing what activities he is ready for at the various levels of his development. By continual observation of his behavior and reactions to situations, the parent can judge fairly well what his child is ready to undertake and enjoy at any given time. While the child of two years is not ready for experiences a three-year-old will welcome and profit from, and the three-year-old's interests and abilities are not those of the four- and five-year-old, age alone does not provide a sufficiently reliable guideline. This is because no two children at any age are identical in all aspects of their personality and development. For example, one two-year-old may ride his tricycle almost as well as most three-year-olds, while another will just push it around and not ride at all. Yet someday they may both play on the same football team. While the one with fewer motor skills at two may verbalize much better than the expert tricycle rider, who can say which child is the more talented? And differences in disposition and temperament do not of themselves reflect differences in ability. One child may need to be protected from rushing into water too deep for him, while another of the same age may need coaxing even to wade in, but both may eventually become equally good swimmers— provided the fearful one is not forced into deep water before he is ready.

This chapter will offer some suggestions on how to observe and evaluate the stages of your child's development through the preschool years. Such informal observations are sufficient for use in guiding and teaching most young children. Only when serious doubts arise as to whether or not your child is growing and developing normally are formal examinations by experts indicated.

Eye-hand coordination develops from month to month and year to year. Many of the activities involving this type of coordination find important application in preparing your child for reading and writing. With the very young child, two to three years of age, you can check with what skill he manipulates objects in his play and in doing small tasks. Note how high he can pile one block upon another before the pile falls down. Observe how well he can place blocks in a box just big enough to hold them all. With what success can he line up his toy cars or place them on the track? How accurately does he place knives, forks, and spoons when helping to set the table? Have him try to throw a soft ball to you from a distance of four or five feet. Can he catch it when you gently toss it back to him? If this proves too difficult, try a game of "catch" while you both sit on the floor. Have him practice catching the ball when you roll it to him and then try rolling it back to you. Does he readily improve in these various activities with a little practice? Can he hold a crayon and try to draw a line on a piece of paper from one dot to another? A somewhat older child can color the inside of a circle or square although sometimes marking over the line. These are only a few of the eye-hand skills every parent can readily observe. You can think of many others, such as the various manipulations required in dressing and eating. At two, your child can probably undress himself but needs a great deal of help in dressing. Not until around three years of age do most children manage the details of eating at the table without messiness, but much depends on the individual child and even more upon the opportunities and encouragement he has had to practice.

In fact, a child's skill not only in motor but also in

other forms of behavior depends to a large degree upon practice. The child's ability to learn to handle himself on a tricycle cannot be judged if he has never had one to ride. The mother who always dresses and undresses her child of two or three does not know how capable he may be of learning to manage by himself. And, as to verbal ability, a child may be more ready to talk than the parents realize if they had found time to talk with him and to encourage him to try to find the words he needs to express himself. Only the child whose parents continually evaluate his readiness for more experience and manage to provide it will be likely to develop his potentialities. Otherwise his abilities remain undetermined and, therefore, cannot be evaluated.

While eye-hand coordination is developing, parents should notice which hand their child prefers in various activities. By age five, right- or left-handedness will tend to be well established. If your child definitely prefers his left hand for eating, using a crayon or pencil, or manipulating other objects, do not insist upon changing him to the right hand because this would tend to interfere with his developing skills and might cause undue frustration and even more serious emotional problems.

Speech behavior is a kind of motor activity, as far as the vocal mechanism is concerned. A child tends to talk like his parents. That is, verbal sounds as they develop are coordinated and partly controlled by hearing. "Baby talk" sometimes delights adults but should not be encouraged. Parents can observe the pitch, volume, and quality of their child's speech. Is it too high or low or just median (pitch); is it loud or soft or just in between (volume); and is his voice clear, sweet, or shrill, (quality)? Also, they can note if their child speaks with expression or monotonously. Guidance will help to modify speech in the preferred direction, provided the parents themselves set a good example and also do not inhibit the child from expressing himself naturally by making him unduly self-conscious about the way he talks. Learning to make speech sounds correctly and to talk clearly and readily is essential preparation for learning to read.

Parents can also watch for a gradual increase in the length of time their child will pay attention to various activities of interest to him. The attention span of small children is naturally brief but lengthens as they mature. From two to three years of age the child needs almost constant supervision as he will seldom "stay put" at his play for long, but runs from his toys or sandbox to whatever else attracts his attention, whether or not it is safe for him to do so. By three, this distractibility is much less noticeable and, by five, the child is apt to resent being interrupted when he is doing something he has started and wants to finish. At any age, the child who is interested in an activity will be motivated to stick with it longer. So note how long your child continues to play with a favorite toy or combination of toys. Observe the length of time he will continue on his own to look at pictures in a book, turning pages as he views the pictures and perhaps verbalizing as he does so. And how long will he listen attentively while you are reading or telling a story he likes? Is his attention span increasing?

Thus the parent studies the interests and capacities of his child and learns about how long to expect him to continue to attend to one activity or another. Praise when he is being unusually attentive will help to extend his attention span. When the parent listens carefully to what the child is trying to say, endeavors to get his exact meaning, and then gives a thoughtful answer, he is helping the child to keep his attention on the subject at hand. It is sometimes surprising to discover how long a young child will attend to an activity that offers just the right combination of excitement and variety to appeal strongly to him. But what commands the continued attention of one child may interest another only momentarily, if at all. For example, a musical toy which produces a variety of sounds may hold the undivided attention of some child for longer than could be reasonably expected for his age level, while a track and trains may be the only set of toys that will occupy the attention of another small child for as long as ten or fifteen minutes. The alert parent, by observing what kinds of activity most readily hold the attention of her child, can pick up cues as to what experiences he is now ready for and as to about how long she can expect him to stay with this or that activity. Too often, adults expect children to pay attention longer than they are able to. This is particularly true when a child is required to perform some unwelcome task. With understanding and encouragement, the child will gradually learn to be more attentive. The child with the longer attention span has a distinct advantage when it comes to learning to read.

Parents can evaluate the stages of language growth through which the child passes from ages two to five and beyond. They will note a rather rapid increase in vocabulary and in the use of sentences. Even the very young child responds correctly to many words and short sentences before using them in his speech. At all preschool ages, the number of words a child uses in talking is much smaller than those he can understand when he hears them. But even his speaking vocabulary may include 2,500 to 3,500 words by the time he is in kindergarten. He begins to use sentences around two years of age. Some of his first attempts to put words together to express his ideas result in very short and often incomplete sentences. To observe the range and variety of his talk, note not only what he says in talking with you but also how he uses words when playing by himself and with other children. The size and range of spoken vocabulary varies markedly in different children during the preschool years. While some children may be naturally more verbal than others, much depends upon whether or not members of the family find time to talk freely and often with the young child, encouraging him to respond by showing a genuine interest in what he is saying, even when he needs quite a bit of help in expressing himself.

There are many other aspects of behavior which the parent will do well to observe in evaluating his child's growth and development. Given the opportunity, the child will begin to recognize some objects in pictures at around two years of age and will enjoy learning to respond to them in simple ways, as by saying "bow-wow" for the dog or by pretending to eat the orange. He likes repetition and delights in seeing over and over again pictures which have become familiar to him and having rhymes and stories repeated many times. Gradually, he learns to really "read" pictures, to enjoy longer stories, and to make up stories of his own suggested by the pictures.

At two years, your child is improving in wrist action and in using crayons but does not always watch his hand movements. Not until around four does he hold a crayon or brush as adults do. By that time he is attempting to draw pictures of objects, some of which will be recognizable to adults. He is also modeling clay to represent something which he definitely has in mind and may treasure what he has made and gladly tell you about it. Also, he can now cut a line on a piece of paper with scissors, and can conceive of and build complicated arrangements with blocks, such as a barn and farmyard or a garage. He is still interested in playing with water and can now fill and empty containers without so much spilling. Such play is now apt to be a part of some plan he has made, such as building a pond in the sand for his boat or serving "tea" for the dolls and members of the family. Only by carefully noting these developments in ideas and the skills needed to carry them out, can the parent know his child well enough to intelligently provide opportunities for logical next steps in his growth experience.

Parents want their children to be generous and to share their toys and possessions, but this is often too difficult for the two- and three-year-old. Understanding the strong feeling of ownership common to children at these ages, the parent will make proper allowance for his young child's possessiveness. By three years of age, the child is more often willing to let others use his toys, and this ability to share can be gently encouraged. He is still possessive of his clothes and takes pride in those he especially likes. The four-year-old is apt to become very fond of his teddy bear or other stuffed animal or perhaps a doll and may talk with it as a companion. Between three and four, imaginary playmates become very real to some children, and their presence should be respected by the parents, knowing that they will be replaced in the course of time by living companions. By four, children have become interested in pennies and other small coins and like to save them but have little or no idea of their worth and may not want to part with any of them to buy anything. These and many other aspects of your child's ever-expanding range of interest and attitudes toward them, when carefully observed, can greatly enrich your understanding of his changing needs.

As your child reaches five years of age, you will find that he has developed markedly in many ways. He speaks clearly and adequately and can understand and follow directions of various kinds. His drawings are more creative, for he chooses beforehand what he will draw and the result is in line with his choice. In general, he now likes to finish a task which he has begun and usually does so with less dawdling than at earlier ages. At five, most children know where they live and can give the exact street address. They can also locate familiar places around the neighborhood. Most five-year-olds are fairly independent in doing many everyday tasks such as washing, dressing, and eating. They can carry out unaided a number of simple household tasks, such as setting the table, emptying a wastebasket, or picking up toys and putting them where they belong. At this age, the child loves to run errands, especially to a nearby neighbor, and he is eager and ready for new experiences outside the home. But he probably still lacks some of the finer coordinations and other abilities needed for success in learning to read and write.

From two to five, parents will note that their child is developing an increasing interest in trips outside the home: going to the park to use play equipment and to be with other children; visiting the zoo; watching trains go by or planes at the airport; watching workmen building a house or using power equipment on the streets; or walking around at the harbor and on the beach to look at the boats, the waves or ripples, and the swimmers. He also has more and more to say about what he is seeing, more questions to ask, and afterward more often spontaneously tells others where he went and what he saw.

During these early years, when their child is developing so rapidly in his behavior—verbal, motor, and social —parents who know what to look for and how to evaluate what they see will find much that is exciting and will become enthusiastic and competent teachers. They will learn to size up their child's stage of development so that they will not expect too much from him but also will see that he has full opportunity to experience and enjoy whatever he is ready for. Such parents will know that it is not enough merely to provide the toys, arrange for the excursions, and see that their child is safely cared for. They will spend time with him out of choice and arrange with pleasure the many shared activities. They will not forget that good communication between parent and child is of prime importance in enabling him to develop language abilities and attitudes essential for learning to read and for adjusting to school.

Some parents find it helpful to keep a record of their observations of their child's growth and development. Especially with the child who develops more slowly than the average, parents tend to become impatient or discouraged. Checking back in the record book may disclose greater gains than they have been aware of. Such informal recording of changes and growth in the child's performance and behavior may also help to identify any problems which may have been developing over a period of time before they are clearly recognized. There is no preferred form or outline for parents to use in recording their observations and their evaluations of their child's progress. Some will like to use a five year line-a-day diary, even though they do not make a practice of daily entries. A record book set up in this form facilitates a quick appraisal of the child's development from year to year. Others will prefer a plain notebook with larger pages and may choose to divide up the space into a small column at the left for entering dates and large columns to follow, each to bear a selected topic heading, such as motor development, speech, health, play. A special space may be allotted to periodic evaluations. In any case, all entries should be dated.

In summary, each child develops at his own rate and in his own way. Much of his development depends directly upon the wisdom with which his parents provide him with opportunities for doing and learning that are suited to his readiness at any given time. To do this, parents need to spend time with their child and to observe and evaluate carefully just how he is progressing. When parents do their job well, there is every likelihood that, upon entering first grade, their child will be ready and eager to learn to read and will adapt quickly and happily to the entire school situation.

Chapter 4.
Everyday Experiences in the Home

Parents may underestimate the value of the child's day-by-day experiences in the home as preparation for reading. One would hardly expect a boy to want to make the Little League ball team who had never enjoyed such competitive play as tag or hide-and-seek and had never owned a ball or learned to throw and catch as well as most of his playmates. Similarly, a parent can expect his child to do well in learning to read only when he has had a range of experience sufficient to provide reading readiness. These experiences will enable him to carry on a conversation, to look at pictures and tell about them, and to be familiar with many of the subjects he will be reading about in his primer. Also, he will have developed feeling of self-confidence, enthusiasm for new ventures, ability to follow directions, perseverance, and ease in relating to his teacher and classmates. These and related accomplishments are the goals to be sought by his parents who are his first teachers. They can rest assured that when their child is ready to read, he will enjoy doing so. Even under the best of conditions, a few children mature slowly and may not be ready to read upon entering first grade. Teacher and parent will then provide further readiness training.

In this chapter we shall limit discussion to what goes on within the home that can help prepare your child for learning to read.

The very young child, from two to three, enjoys helping his mother and whenever possible his "help" should be welcomed and so directed as to insure him pleasure and satisfaction from his efforts. When he wants to help set the table, he can place the silver around but may not be equal to carrying breakable dishes. In trying to give each member of the family the utensils he will need, the child is beginning to develop the idea of counting. Children of this age are especially interested in the preparation of food and like to watch their mothers cooking. They can take some small part in whatever she is doing, such as handing her the egg beater or frosting a cookie or two. Later, the child will be proud to pass the cookies to others in the family or to guests. These and other shared activities help in the development of motor skills and provide natural opportunities for encouraging conversation and adding to his vocabulary. Other jobs around the house of interest and value to the very young child are putting papers in the wastebasket, wiping up a wet spot on the linoleum, bringing in the milk cartons, shutting the door, getting the newspaper for daddy, and even helping to clean the bathroom and making the beds. Even when what he does has to be done over, his efforts should be rewarded with recognition and approval. Experiencing success in these first ventures is of great importance to the child. The busy parent is tempted just to tell the child to run along and play, but whenever possible she should welcome the child's interest, curiosity, and desire to help, realizing how much can be taught and readily learned while doing things together. Even the very young child will learn to follow directions, develop motor skills, and increase his vocabulary. And, above all, he will be enjoying the companionship of someone he loves, finding pleasure in helping, in learning to do new things, and in the approval received for his efforts and accomplishments. The pattern desired for all future learning is thus being formed.

The very short attention span of the two-year-old gradually lengthens until by three and four, the child will spend quite some time on a single play activity. Ordinarily, when busy at some such play, the child should not be interrupted to help his mother. Nor should grown-ups interfere in what he is doing by giving directions as to the right way to do this or that. They should, of course, show interest, help out when asked, and admire the results. Creative, imaginative play is a growth process in itself. It encourages independence and develops capacity to think, to reason, to put ideas into practice, and to make corrections and improvements.

The three- and four-year-old can begin to take on tasks which they do regularly. Perhaps the first such task should be undressing. Usually the child will delight in doing this and before long, with a little encouragement and frequent reminders, will be learning to hang up his clothes. Dressing is more difficult, but with guidance he will finally master pulling up the zipper, putting a button in its hole, and even tying his shoes. This will give him great pride in accomplishment. At a very early age, he can regularly help in making his bed and in picking up his toys. Putting things in order will not in itself have much meaning for him, but he will be interested in seeing if he can get his toys back on the shelf, and he may like the idea of putting the doll in its bed and his picture books in the bookcase. By four, some children can carry through simple, regular tasks unaided, but others still need the company and co-operation of an adult. The parent must guard against expecting too much of three- and four-year olds, even though at times they may seem quite mature. No child should ever be expected to undertake more than he can do satisfactorily and with pride.

Often it may seem that the young child takes an excessive amount of time to complete a task. It is not natural for a young child to work fast or to concentrate for more than a short period on any task. Although dawdling should not become habitual, the parent should recognize that young children have little concept of time and so are seldom motivated to consider time important in what they are doing. To aid the child in completing a task fairly promptly, incentives may help, as by saying, "When you've finished putting your toys away, we'll be going to the store" or "Then you can have your lunch."

In the course of all the activities in the home in which the child shares, the parents should strive for increasingly good communication between parent and child and between their child and other children and adults. It cannot be stressed too strongly how important verbal facility is to learning how to read. (This is discussed in greater detail in Chapter 6.) Most children ask many questions, including some that are difficult to answer satisfactorily. However, the parents should try to answer all questions. If the parents are too busy at the moment to do so, then care should be taken to tell the child that the question will be answered as soon as possible so the child will not be disappointed and perhaps frustrated. Failure to answer a child's questions may discourage his coming to you when he needs to know something. His natural curiosity about many things may become stifled and his vocabulary development delayed. When, for example, a headline in the newspaper creates excited discussion between his parents and the child asks, "What is it? Tell me," and is put off, the child's curiosity and keen interest remain unsatisfied. What is more, he feels pushed aside by both parents.

Just as the child is included in many of the activities of other members of the family, so should his parents participate in the child's own activities. First of all, they should see that he has play equipment in keeping with his level of development and his interests. Simple toys are best for preschool children. They like blocks, balls, dolls and doll equipment, toy cars and planes, farmyard sets, hand and finger puppets (used especially in telling them stories), simple puzzles, and other toys that can be taken apart, put together, pushed, pulled, wound up, piled up, carried around, or that can play a tune or make noises. The older preschool child may enjoy a few games such as ring toss, picture-card games, and perhaps dominoes and Parcheesi. Many time-honored games require little equipment, such as hide-the-thimble (or any other small object), guessing what object in the room someone is thinking of, or beanbag. Older preschool children also have great fun with a box of clothes for dressing up in high heels, hats, etc. Knowing the parent is nearby, a small child will play happily alone for short periods, which helps to prevent his becoming too dependent on the attention of adults. By four and five, he is ready for more interaction with playmates but still needs a good deal of supervision until he becomes more socially mature. In all his play the thoughtful interest of his parents is of great help in his development. In playing games with their children, parents can begin to teach them to take turns, to play fairly, to try to win but to be good losers, and in general to learn to take their place in the competitions they will encounter in school and elsewhere. In addition, the child will find great enjoyment and stimulus in having those he loves share in whatever interests him at the moment.

All children should have crayons and paper, at first just for scribbling, and later for drawing and coloring. At the younger ages, a pencil is difficult for a child to use—crayons are better. Soon the child will be making designs that are meaningful to him even though they may not be to his parents. He may welcome a chance to talk about what he has put on the paper. While using crayons he is beginning to learn eye-hand coordination. As he grows older he will delight in coloring pictures printed in outline form. This will help him learn to distinguish colors and their appropriate use: green for grass, yellow for the sun, black for smoke from the chimney, etc. In time he will learn the names of the colors in objects around him. Another drawing activity enjoyed by the older child is to connect a series of dots with a line which will outline an object such as an animal, a person, or a house.

Many activities which the parent can devise can provide meaningful activity for the child. A few examples follow: Teach the body parts by touching the child's hands and saying, "Here are your hands. Jane has wonderful hands. Here is your nose. Jane has a wonderful nose." In a similar manner, continue the chant with head, eyes, ears, neck, arms, fingers, thumb, legs, knees, feet, and hair. After some repetitions on different days, ask Jane to point to her ear, nose, etc. Encourage her to say, "This is my nose," as she points to it. Later, she can learn to answer correctly when you ask, "Where is my nose?"

Another home exercise for a somewhat older child that will help to develop vocabulary involves learning the differences between sizes of objects. Cut out squares of paper or cardboard of about one inch, two inches, and three inches. Then, tell your child, "This is the smallest. This is the bigger. And this is the biggest," putting them in order of size. Then, mix up the squares and ask the child to find the smallest and then to put the squares in order of size. After this has been learned, add two more squares of differing sizes and again ask the child to identify the smallest and the biggest. Do similar exercises with other objects such as stones, spoons, or blocks.

The older preschool child can learn to identify figures of different shapes and to name them. Cut out of cardboard a triangle, a square, and a rectangle about two inches high. Call attention to the different shapes as you name them. Then, describe each by showing that the square has four sides and that every side is the same length. Talk similarly about the rectangle—it also has four sides but two are shorter than the other two—pointing them out. Then, describe the triangle, noting that it has only three sides. Repeat the exercise on successive days until the child can identify each figure and tell you why it is a triangle, a square, or a rectangle. Then, draw the figures on paper and help the child to recognize them. Next, send him on a search within the house to look for articles with these shapes. This game can be played out of doors as well using, of course, far larger objects. (Rectangular buildings, square houses.)

Your child can also have fun with circles. Draw a circle about two inches in diameter and ask what shape it is. Most children recognize the shape of a circle at a very early age. Demonstrate how your child can make a circle by touching the ends of thumb and index finger and a big circle by holding his arms out and touching the tips of the fingers of each hand. Then, show several objects that are circular in shape: a ring, a ball, a plate, the face of the clock, the top of a cup or glass, etc. Ask him to draw pictures of circular objects such as the sun, an orange, a face with round eyes. You can also cut out some circles of paper of different sizes and, as you did with the squares, ask which is the biggest, the smallest, and which of two is bigger.

Another parent-child play makes use of a "magic box" to give experience in naming objects and talking about them. Place in a box a number of objects that are commonplace in any home, such as a spoon, a toy car, a crayon, a key, a flashlight, a nail, a little box, an apple, a leaf from a bush or tree, and/or other small objects. Ask your child to reach in the box and take out something. Then, ask him to name it, and tell what it is used for. Four- and five-year-olds will love this game and with a judicious selection of objects to put in the box, many younger children will like it, too. The parent should help with things not named correctly and when necessary will explain their use, as well as give other uses for the object.

Another game for the young child is to present him with situations in which he can discover that something is out of place or is being done incorrectly. For example, put a shoe on the wrong foot, a jacket on backwards, draw a picture with the sun on the ground or with milk being poured on the table beside the glass. Ask the child what is wrong and let him help fix it so that it is right. Children are not only amused by this game but are enthusiastic as well because it stimulates them to observe carefully and to suggest corrections to be made.

Growing house plants can be interesting and instructive for your child. He can help put some pebbles and water in a dish and place a narcissus bulb among the pebbles so that the bottom of the bulb is in the water. The bulb will start to sprout before long. Together, you can replenish the water as needed. Your child will enjoy watching this plant grow and bloom with a rich fragrance. Another satisfactory plant to use is a sweet potato. Stick some toothpicks (about four) in the sides of the potato and rest them on the top of a glass of water so that the bottom end of the potato is in the water and the other end points upward. Set it in a light place, and in about two weeks your child will see the beginnings of roots and leaves. It is exciting for young children to watch a plant grow. Explain that light on the leaves makes food for the plant to grow larger. Let him care for the plant within his ability, and welcome his questions about growing things. You might also let him plant three or four beans in a flower pot. Keep the soil moist, and watch for the growth. You can let him pull up the first bean to show above the surface so that he can see how it has opened up when the sprouts start. Later on, when he will be reading about growing things, he will do so with greater interest and understanding because of his own experience at home with plants.

Young children are fascinated by animals unless they are so large or unfriendly as to be frightening. The child growing up on a farm or in the country will probably have had several pets of his own and be familiar with a number of domestic and wild animals by the time he will be reading about some of them in his primer and in the readers to follow. In urban areas parents may find it difficult to give their preschool children the pleasure and advantages of pets in the home and may have to rely on trips to the zoo to acquaint the young child with live animals and birds. (See Chapter 5.) Even when parents can keep a pet, much of the responsibility for its care must rest on older members of the family, and the safety of the small child must always be considered. Within these limitations, parents should try to find some way for their preschool child to have a pet. Even a canary or fish in a bowl will give him some of the firsthand experience he needs with living creatures, but a pet he can play with, such as a puppy or a kitten, would be much more meaningful. He can feel happily superior to a small pet, will want to protect and care for it, will make many observations about its behavior and may become very fond of it, even before he has learned to care very much about children his own age.

Between four and five, as your child approaches kindergarten age, he will be more assertive than at three, ask more questions, and be reaching out for new experiences. While much of the time he will be very active, he will also be able to sit quietly for rather long periods when working on some project which interests him. He will probably talk a lot, trying out big words, making up silly ones, and pursuing a subject until he is satisfied as to what actually happened. He will want to know how things work and why others do this or that. The parent will note that he has better organized his play activities and that he uses his imagination with ease to create whatever he wants out of simple materials. He likes to exaggerate and to dramatize. This is the time to expand his experiences by trips (as described in Chapter 5), to arrange more play with other children of about his age, and to increase the variety of activities in the home. He can be given more privileges and responsibilities, but his energy, enthusiasm, and lack of maturity may lead to trouble unless a parent keeps in close touch with what he is doing and maintains necessary limits.

The four-year-old will spend some time looking at picture books by himself and is more ready to be read to than earlier. He loves songs, some of which he may be able to sing, and likes to listen to his favorite records. He likes rhymes and rhythmic games. He may be interested in learning to recognize letters in children's alphabet books. But he is too busy with new experiences and new ideas to care for artificial "reading readiness workbooks." His time is better spent in a full program of natural activities within and around the home where he is learning and growing at a rapid rate.

Learning to count can begin at about four years of age. Always use objects in counting. Start with two objects and gradually move to three and four and on up to ten. Some children can go beyond counting to ten by the time they are five years of age.

Although your child at five is not ready for first grade reading books, he does need books. (Books are discussed in greater detail in Chapter 10.) He should have a few books of his own. He will know one from another by the pictures which will recall to him many of the stories he has had read to him. A special shelf or a small bookcase of his own will add to his pride of ownership, as will his name written on the flyleaf of each book. Also, he can now help choose new picture and story books which he would like to examine and have read to him. In addition to telling and reading stories to him at odd times, as should have been done since he was very young, there is much to be said in favor of now setting up a regular daily storytime. This might be just before he goes to bed or perhaps with his father while mother is preparing the evening meal or whenever it fits in best to the family schedule. During this special time, reading and telling stories, conversation, and a game or two can be enjoyed by both child and parent.

Television tends to become a fascinating experience for children between the ages of three and six. A number of programs provide good educational material. For instance, the program *Sesame Street*, prepared by the Children's Television Workshop, is designed specifically to prepare the child for reading. In viewing this daily program, children learn about themselves and the world around them. Programs suitable for young children should be selected with some care by the parents, especially avoiding frightening scenes of violence. Animal and nature pictures, animated cartoons, and some simple stories about the adventures of young children are appropriate. Perennial favorites include *Lassie* and *Disneyland*, although some of the latter programs are designed for older children. The viewing of TV by preschool children does increase their vocabulary. It has been demonstrated that children who have been viewers of television during the preschool years have acquired a vocabulary about one year beyond that of children who have not had television experience. This more advanced vocabulary will help the children who have watched TV to get off to a fast start in reading when they enter first grade.

The greatest improvement in learning correct speech sounds occurs between the ages of two and three. But further gains take place in successive years up through the primary grades—and beyond. The vowel sounds come more easily than consonant sounds, especially the consonant blends, such as *ch, tr, sh, th, wh, bl, cl, cr,* and *br.* The parent can do much to help his child develop correct pronunciation of letter sounds. While "baby talk" may seem cute, it should not be encouraged. The child arriving in first grade and still using baby talk is distinctly handicapped in learning to read. So, a continuing effort should be made in the home to help the child eliminate baby talk and employ correct usage. With proper guidance, your child will have acquired about 88 percent of correct pronunciation of letter sounds when reading begins at about age six. This is an average. Some children will do better, some not quite so well. Progress in learning to read is heavily dependent upon good oral language.

The average length of sentence used by your child of course increases as he grows older. The average three-year-old will talk in sentences of about four words. By the time he is six years old, he will be using six or seven words in many of his sentences. This development, along with improved pronunciation and grammatical accuracy, can be aided by the parents. Any experience that encourages the child to talk in communicating with them and with others provides excellent stimulation for the language development so important in reading.

Every parent should realize that while the majority of children will progress in language development so that they will be ready to start learning to read soon after six years of age, this is not necessarily the case for every individual child. Some children will be ready to read before six years of age, many at about six, and a few will not be ready until later. The child's language develops according to the language he hears at home and the kind and amount of help and encouragement he receives from other members of the family. And, as every parent knows, no two children have exactly equal abilities. Individual differences of many kinds will be present among the children entering first grade, as pointed out in Chapter 9. But, with informed guidance by the parents, most children will be ready to learn to read when they enter first grade.

Reading is based upon the oral vocabulary learned through experiences of various kinds. Many of these experiences can and should occur in the home. The parents who wish to prepare their children for reading can do much to promote reading readiness. The experiences provided and fostered by the parent should be as informal as possible. They should not set up any regular "school" program in an attempt to hasten reading readiness. Instead, parents should offer incentives which encourage the child to ask for the fun of "helping" with home activities, of being read to, and of learning all sorts of new things. The observant parent who spends time with his child will be able to judge what is within the child's ability and inclination at any given time and will not try to force his development. It will not be difficult to arouse his interest in activities when he is ready for them. Interest breeds motivation and when motivated, the child will participate and learn. Parents should be patient, understanding, and helpful. Approve the efforts of your child even though the results are imperfect.

Keep in mind that vocabulary knowledge and facility in verbal usage are highly important in learning to read. Also remember that if your child goes to kindergarten, you should still continue to provide growth experiences at home. In fact, the activities in the home should serve as a rich supplement to the learning experiences in school through kindergarten, first grade, and beyond. (See Chapters 5, 6, and 10.)

With adequate teaching and guidance during the preschool years, almost certainly your child will not only be ready for reading about the time he enters first grade, but also will be eager to learn and will adjust happily to the total school situation.

Chapter 5.
Experiences Outside the Home

Experience which provides your child with new concepts and new vocabulary is the very core from which reading readiness develops. Well-chosen new experiences will delight him, stimulate his thinking, and arouse his curiosity. What he may do and learn in the home was discussed in the preceding chapter. Equally important are experiences outside the home. It is not enough just to see pictures of animals in the jungle or at the zoo or just to hear stories and songs about sailing a boat. A nucleus of firsthand experience is needed for the child to be able to appreciate related happenings when he sees pictures of them or hears about them from someone else. The young child is just beginning to learn about his world. He needs to see for himself more animals than just the family cat and larger bodies of water than the bathtub will hold.

As soon as the child is walking and is fairly steady on his feet, he is ready to explore the yard at his home. He will find pebbles, ants, and worms, and many small things in which most grown-ups have long since lost interest. But they can share his interest and try to see the world through his eyes which are so much nearer the ground than theirs. Before long, the young child can have a small part in planting flower seeds, watching the plants come up, watering the garden, and picking the flowers. He can also help gather up the lawn clippings or the dry leaves. Helping in the yard will be more fun for him and he will feel more important if he has a few tools and a little equipment of his own, such as a small watering can, a spade, a rake, and a cart or child's wheelbarrow or at least a basket for carrying things around. A sandbox or a pile of dirt where he can play with his pail, shovel, dump truck, and even his watering can will initiate imaginative play differing from what he does in the house. And soon he will be learning to ride his tricycle in the driveway and on the walks. But there are limits here, too, for he is not permitted to go into the street and any attempt to do so must bring prompt action from the watchful parent. If calling him back is not sufficient, he should be taken away from his lovely yard into the house for a time. For the child living in a house with no yard, the parents will need to make special provisions, such as arranging frequent trips to the park, the beach, and the countryside.

Walks around the neighborhood with one of his parents will yield much of interest to the young child. In crossing streets, he will begin to learn the meaning of stop signs and to watch for cars coming around the corner. He will enjoy standing to look at traffic going by and soon will be distinguishing between trucks and passenger cars. He may meet strange dogs or cats and see other children on the street or playing in their yards. There may be a bridge to cross or a hill to climb. The school where older children go will become more than a strange word to him. And stopping at the corner store to make some small purchase which he can eat or carry home will be exciting. If the parent will become an active participant in these little adventures, answering questions, pointing out and explaining objects and places of interest, and whenever possible letting the child set his own pace, pausing here and there to watch or examine whatever captures his attention, and after they get home talking about what they have seen and done, the child will be adding new words and many bits of information to his small but rapidly increasing store of knowledge.

For high adventure the young child does not need to be taken on expensive trips. Adults tend to forget what simple experiences they enjoyed when they were very young. For example, small children often find nighttime out-of-doors strange and exciting but not too scary when accompanied by a parent on a short walk. Flashlight in hand, the child explores familiar places that at night seem new and mysterious. There is darkness all around, but the moon and the stars are bright; light shines from windows and comes up the street along with sounds of cars. Flashing his own light, he can make bright spots on familiar objects. Perhaps he will see eyes shining out of the darkness and will find that they belong to his own cat. There are sounds, too. A bird chirps in a dark tree. Footsteps are heard. Is it a man or a woman? How can you tell in the darkness? There is a rumbling sound in the sky above. His father says it is a plane and that the whistle they hear from faraway is made by a train. Perhaps he recognizes the fragrance on the night air from a bush in the yard of syringa, lilac, or jasmine, or he may smell a skunk for the first time. The warm touch of his father's hand makes all this safe and fascinating. There will be much to talk about after such a venture into the night. Where has the sun gone anyway? Can he go to the moon someday? What makes lights? Why was the grass wet? Where was the cat going? What does a skunk look like, and why does he smell so bad? New sights and sounds and other sensations require new words if you are going to talk about them, and the eager child learns them rapidly in conversation with interested parents.

In your program of preparing your child for reading, trips outside the neighborhood can have high educational value. The very young child will like best short trips to parks or to a nearby countryside to see animals on a farm or just to walk by a brook in the woods or among flowers in an open field. But by three years of age, most children can also enjoy and profit from a great variety of excursions especially when, before going, they are prepared for what they will see, their interest is aroused, and some of their questions answered. Many mothers have to take their preschool children along with them on errands to the post office, store, or market. With a little thought, these trips can be so planned as to provide their child with meaningful experiences.

For example, take the trip to the post office. The child should already know about sending and receiving letters and packages through the mail. Perhaps a postman comes to the house or the family mailbox each day, or his parents may get the mail from the post office, and he hears talk about going there and sees what they bring back. Possibly he has himself received a gift or a card through the mail. Before taking him to the post office to see what goes on there, the parent should tell him about the clerks who sell stamps, weigh packages, and sort mail, the individual letter boxes, and the places to put outgoing mail in slots inside the post office or in large mailboxes outside. When approaching the building, point out the American flag flying outside and try to give your child some idea of the postal service being conducted by our government. At the rear of the building, you may be able to show him mail trucks loading or unloading bags of mail, and there may be postmen in uniform starting out on their rounds. Inside, your child can watch people bringing packages and letters to the windows or receiving them there or taking them out of their individual boxes. If you have mail to go, let your child put it in the slot, showing him which one is for airmail. If you were to count up the number of new words your child hears and begins to use in planning for and taking a trip to the post office, you would no doubt be surprised. And he will also be gaining new concepts and quite a bit of practical information.

Similar trips, whether made in connection with errands the parent has to do or has planned just for the child, will widen his horizon and help to prepare him for what he will read and study about when he goes to school. Even before then, what he sees in his picture books at home and on television and what he hears in stories read or told to him and in the conversation of grown-ups will immediately take on more meaning as he learns firsthand about places and people and what is going on in the community where he lives. Places to take your child, most of which are probably within easy reach, include the following:

GROCERY STORE	POLICE STATION
PET SHOP	NATURAL HISTORY MUSEUM
BANK	CHURCH
GAS STATION	LIBRARY
POST OFFICE	CONSTRUCTION PROJECTS
RAILROAD STATION	LAUNDROMAT
AIRPORT	FARM
DAIRY	GREENHOUSE
DEPARTMENT STORE	CITY PARKS
FIRE STATION	SCHOOL
ZOO	HARBOR OR DOCKS

To the list should be added the place where the father works. While even very young children become familiar with many of their mother's homemaking activities, what their father does at work is apt to remain little known to them. The child so fortunate as to live on a farm does not have to cope with this mystery. Even before all the words are in his speaking vocabulary, he knows by repeated observation that his father milks the cows by hand or milking machine, feeds the farm animals, plows the field and the garden, plants the seeds, cuts the hay, and so forth. But, when the father works away from home, parents should arrange for their child to find out more about what he does between the time he leaves home in the morning and returns at night. This is best done by occasionally taking him to his father's place of work. Some thought and planning will be required to make such an excursion as meaningful as it should be to the young child unless the nature of the father's occupation can be readily viewed and understood by him, such as operating a crane or working as a dentist. If the father works at a desk in an office, he may not be able to explain to his preschool child much of what his work is all about. But he can let the child sit at his desk and draw on a piece of paper taken from the desk drawer, and perhaps can put in a phone call to Mother or to some other member of the family so that the child can carry on a conversation from Daddy's desk phone. Then, if there is a dictaphone, making a little record of the child's voice and playing it back to him will greatly surprise and delight him. He can meet a few of the other office workers, get a drink from the water cooler or the soft drink machine, and perhaps watch the telephone switchboard and ride on the elevator. Such a small excursion can become a big event in his life and will strengthen rapport between father and child.

Similarly, when his mother is employed outside the home, the child needs to know where she goes and what she does. This becomes all the more important when he does not altogether like to have her leave him in the care of someone else when she goes to work. After he has visited her place of employment, he will be more interested in hearing about what she did at work on a particular day or about incidents which occurred there, for now he will be better able to understand what she tells him.

There are many specials occasions for small, or not so small, trips for the child. Some are connected with holidays, such as going to see the Fourth-of-July fireworks or Santa Claus and Christmas decorations at the stores or a special program at school. Preschool children accompanied by a parent can take part in the activities on Hallowe'en. An open-air band concert or a short boat ride can provide special outings, and the circus may come to town. Then there are invitations to birthday parties or an egg roll at Easter. Family vacations or visits to the grand-parents or other relatives can be anticipated, enjoyed, and talked about afterward.

On long trips in the car, the grown-ups can help to occupy the children by devising simple games based on what they see along the way. For example, if the child is too young to count very well, mother and child can count the animals seen on one side of the highway, while the father or older child counts those on the other side. Count-ing kinds or colors of cars is another game, but no games should last too long. Allowances should be made for leisurely stops at highway rest areas and gas stations.

Preparing your child for an excursion of any kind should be done informally. The plans may very well in-clude an element of surprise and awaken eager anticipa-tion. When feasible, the choice of a destination may be based upon some circumstance which has aroused in the child a special interest or curiosity. For example, after seeing and hearing a fire engine go by, his excitement and questions have led to talk about fires and how firemen put them out. This is a good time to plan a trip to a fire station. In preparing your child for this trip, tell him why we have fire stations, describe the different kinds of vehicles the firemen use—the chief's car, the pumping truck, the ladder truck—and how the sirens serve to clear the traffic out of the way. Explain that firemen are on duty day and night, and tell how they get word of a fire. When you and your child go to the fire station, the men on duty will be glad to show the equipment, explain its use, and answer questions. The experience will be an exciting one for your child and for several days after he gets home, he will like to tell about it and ask more questions. Often at the dinner table, young children feel left out of the conversation. The parent who has just taken him on a trip can help him share their experience with other members of the family. All may then join in comparing what they recall of what they did and saw on similar trips.

The dates when the circus will be in town limit the choice of when to go to it. Does the child know the word *circus*? If he has seen pictures of clowns and circus animals in one of his picture books, look at them again with him, explaining them in more detail and inviting questions. If no such pictures are available, tell about some of the animals he will see, such as elephants and monkeys, and mention that he has seen them at the park or the zoo. Describe what part such animals play in the circus, mentioning also that dogs and horses will probably run, jump, and do tricks.

Talking over an excursion afterward with your child and encouraging him to tell others about it can greatly increase its value to him as a learning experience. He needs practice in using all the new words he became acquainted with on the trip. As he is encouraged to think over and relate what he saw and did, no doubt he will have more questions to ask, such as, "How can people walk high up on a wire, Daddy?" Also, you will have a good opportunity to clear up any misunderstandings and to fill in some of the gaps in his information. What he has learned on the trip can also be reinforced by following it up with a judicious selection of pictures and stories relating to it. Some children will spontaneously relive their excursion experiences in their play by setting up an imaginary circus or pretending to be firemen putting out fires with their toy cars used as fire trucks. Some others will enjoy this type of play when it is suggested to them.

Children of almost any age love picnics at the seashore, mountains, lake, or state and national parks. However, a child under three may be just as well satisfied with a picnic in the backyard or just down the street at the park where he is often taken to play. But older children find more distant places exciting and interesting, for there is so much to see on the way and to explore at the picnic grounds. While planning a picnic, talk with your child about where you plan to go and what kinds of country you will be passing through on the way. It is likely that you will be going off the freeway or turnpike and pass some farms. You can describe the kinds of buildings he will probably see on a farm, such as the main farmhouse, the big barn and barnyard, perhaps a silo, and probably some smaller buildings, such as a chicken house. Talk with him about what each is used for. Ask him what animals he should be looking for, giving him any help he may need to name the obvious ones. Along the way you will probably see some orchards and may pass through woods. Starting with the kinds of trees he already knows in his own yard and along his street and including the fir trees he sees at Christmas time, tell him about a few other kinds to watch for. Does he know about fruit trees? Or does he only think of apples and oranges and other kinds of fruit as coming from the store?

Even a small child can help plan the food for the picnic. Perhaps he can be given the choice of taking hot dogs or hamburgers, or pick out his favorite soft drink to take along. The older child can count out the paper plates and cups and the eating utensils, and help to pack them. He can get his ball, his swimsuit, sweater, and whatever else is appropriate for him to take along and help carry things out to the car. At the picnic site, he can help unload the car. If wood is needed for a campfire, he will enjoy collecting twigs and small pieces for kindling. If you are to do some fishing, let him help assemble the fishing rod. Show him how to hold the rod, and explain how he'll know when he gets a bite. Do not be surprised or find fault if he loses interest before this happens. You might then suggest he go to help set the table, and then call him back when someone catches a fish so that he can watch it being pulled in. After the picnic meal, playing catch with the ball or going for a walk are things both you and the children can enjoy together. A trip to the beach affords all sort of opportunities for play and learning. There are sandcastles to build, the chance to learn how to swim, and talks about how the ocean surrounds us and connects us with other countries. Always remember that a small child's attention span is short and that a little goes a long way when it comes to instruction of any sort. And some children take to ocean-swimming or wading immediately, while others are terrified by the waves and noise. This can be true of the same child from one year to the next. Never force a child to learn how to swim.

On the return trip there will be new sights to enjoy and talk about. Even though you return by the same route, the roadside viewed from the opposite direction will appear different. During the next few days there is bound to be talk about what happened on the picnic. Be sure to include your child in such talk so that he can practice using the new additions to his vocabulary, express any new ideas, and get answers to whatever questions he may ask.

Your child has seen planes in the air and on the ground and in all likelihood has seen toy planes as well. And he has certainly seen pictures of planes in books and magazines and on television. But very likely he has never been on a plane or visited an airport. To prepare him for a trip to the airport, the parent might enter into an imaginary journey with him by plane to visit someone living at a distance whom he would like to see. Let him set up an airport with his blocks or with pieces of furniture, so that there will be a ticket counter, a waiting room, a restaurant, and perhaps a shop or two. Dolls can serve at the ticket counter and as porters, waitresses, and store clerks, or some of these functionaries can just be imagined. Packing a little bag, driving to the airport, buying a ticket, boarding the plane, leaving it at his destination, being met by friends, and the return flight home can all be part of the play, a kind of make-believe most young children thoroughly enjoy. This play will give the parent an excellent opportunity to introduce new vocabulary, to add to what little his child knows about air travel, and to arouse his keen interest in seeing for himself what a real airport is like and what goes on there. If the parent has provided some preparation, his child will be much more knowledgeable about what he sees on the trip and will actually see more. All his questions will tend to be more pertinent. Probably he will engage in more informed play with his toys and blocks after visiting the airport, and this will give him a good chance to recall and apply what he has learned.

A similar trip can be made to the railroad depot, preferably at a time when a passenger train is due. On drives in the car, the child has no doubt seen freight trains, and there will probably be some freight cars near the station on sidetracks, even if no trains happen to be passing through.

By the time your child is about ready to enter first grade, or even before that, he will have learned a number of things about money. Coins are no longer merely shiny trinkets to play with and put in his bank, for he has learned that he can buy things with them. He can distinguish between pennies, nickels, and dimes and may even recognize a quarter, but he is apt to call any folding money "a dollar bill." While he cannot add up the value of his coins, he may know which one will buy what he wants from the Good Humor man or how much he needs to get an ice-cream cone at the corner store.

It is not too soon to introduce him to your bank, for he has heard you talk about going there, putting money in the bank or getting some out, and has often seen you get out your checkbook and write a check. But all he really knows as yet about banks is probably that he has one, such as a piggy bank, into which he puts his coins. Starting with what he knows, you can begin to enlarge the meaning of the word *bank*. You can tell him that your bank is a whole building and point out some bank buildings when you pass them. Explain that while it is the bank you use, lots of other people use it, too, and that is why it is so big. Your child will have no difficulty understanding, when you point it out, that people want to keep their money in a safe place but where they can get it when they need to buy something or pay bills. While the use of checks is a little complicated for such a young child to fully comprehend, you can surely give him the general idea. Perhaps you can also explain that when you are not using all your money, some banks are ready to borrow it and pay you interest in return for its use. You might also assure him that when he is older he can have his own savings account at a bank and get interest on it. Before going with him to the bank, you can also mention the safe-deposit boxes for keeping valuable papers. Upon arrival at the bank, call his attention to the tellers and what they do, and perhaps cash a check or deposit some money. Point out the safe or vault where all the money is locked up at night, and the safe-deposit boxes (perhaps you have one), and also the clerks who are working on the accounts of the depositors. After returning home, talk over with your child what he has learned and try to clear up any misunderstandings. From time to time from then on, tell him about any of your money transactions that will help to keep fresh in his mind what he has been learning about the use of banks in handling money.

There will be some trips that your child will want to make again and again that can be repeated many times with pleasure and profit, such as visiting the zoo or the natural history museum. As with other trips, the parent should tell his child what he will see before he goes for the first time and, while there, guide him and tell him about the animals or exhibits. Then, on succeeding days, what has been seen and learned can be followed up by talking it over and having recourse to picture books and stories about wildlife. In preparation for subsequent trips, the parent may have to do a little research on his own so that he will know more about the natural habitat and manner of life of various animals, birds, reptiles, and fish in which his child is developing a growing interest.

Parents who teach their child well about the world outside the home do so with enjoyment and enthusiasm. There is no need for set periods for instructions, questions and answers, and review. Most young children are full of energy and, when provided with new experiences outside the home in keeping with their level of development, will respond with eagerness and curiosity. Some parents, it is true, seem to be natural teachers who have no trouble in sharing their child's enthusiasm and in capitalizing on each of his new experiences by using it as a means of learning. But all parents who will spend time with their child, talk with him, listen to him, help him explore new and exciting places, and learn to understand whatever he is ready to find out about, can expect success in preparing him for the reading and studying years which are ahead.

Chapter 6.
The Role of Language Facility

The greater your child's ability to comprehend material presented in oral form and the greater his proficiency in the use of oral language, the more ready he will be for success in beginning reading. Various factors are involved in the improvement of verbal facility. Some of these have to do with learning to listen to stories told or read, and others with developing the ability to take part in conversations. In order to understand what is said and to have something to say, a child is dependent upon whatever experiences he has had. From a very early age, all children should have experiences in a variety of sensory situations including seeing, smelling, hearing, touching, and tasting. Often these experiences in themselves provide opportunity for verbal exchange between parent and child which will increase the child's ability to express feelings and other sensations in words.

To say to your child, "Talk to me," may only inhibit his speaking, particularly if he is under some feelings of tension. Growth of language expression occurs most rapidly in a relaxed, friendly atmosphere. The smallest effort of your young child to tell you something should be accepted with pleasure. Try to shape the situation so that he will keep trying without feeling urged. When you discover what he is trying to say, talk it over with him with some rephrasing on your part so that he may learn several ways to express the same idea. For example, your child of around three may say something like this: "I want, I don't want, do I have to, one rubber is gone." Instead of just saying, "You must wear your rubbers or stay in the house," you might respond with, "Do you mean you can't find one rubber? You know there are puddles of water in the yard. What were you going to do outside?" The child may then speak of sailing his toy boat or walking through the puddles. The conversation could well continue for a few moments about fun playing in the water, how chilly it is outside even though the sun is shining, his not wanting to get his feet cold and wet, and needing help to find that other rubber or boot. Once it is found, he is on his way after a helpful and agreeable talking-over of his problem with a mother who understands. He may have learned a new word or two and has had a little practice in putting together the words he already knows so that they will express clearly what he had been having difficulty in saying. Even a child who is normally talkative may be blocked in trying to speak when he cannot sort out his ideas and does not know how to express the relationships between them. Parents can help in conversation to clarify words and meanings so that their child will gain facility in putting his thoughts into words.

Listening to stories read or told and encouraging your child to tell his own stories promotes verbal facility. (See Chapter 7.) Improvement in his use of sentences depends upon hearing language well-spoken in the home and upon practice with some guidance by the parents. The breaks between sentences develop gradually. Language games and exercises help the child to improve sentence structure. Looking at pictures with your child to see what is happening in them can help to serve this purpose. For instance, with a picture of a boy and a dog, he may start by saying, "The boy is playing." You can then ask if he is playing by himself, which may lead him to reply, "No, he is playing with his dog." Further comments and questions by you are in order as long as your child's attention is held by that particular picture. He should feel free to turn the page to a new picture whenever he wants. The young child can also play a game with you of completing sentences. You are to start a sentence, such as, "A little girl can. . . ." and then ask her what comes next. You may have to explain that she can choose what the little girl can do. Her reply may be, "A little girl can wear a pink dress." This can readily lead to other related questions, such as "and what is it that a little boy can. . . .?" Word games like this can help your child develop sentence sense.

The five- and six-year-old can develop word-meaning from the context of the sentence. For instance, suppose that your child is listening to a story which he understands readily until he hears this sentence, "the cowboy was riding a mustang." He has never heard the word *mustang,* but he does not need to be told that it is a kind of horse. However, he will like to hear more about mustangs and will be interested to learn that they are small, sometimes wild, horses of the American plains descended from horses brought by explorers from Spain. This information will very likely lead him to inquire further about any other kinds of horses, with the result that his initial concept of the meaning of the word *horse* will be enriched.

Imitation of the parents' speech is a common way for children to improve their own speech. If your child has difficulty in making certain sounds, you may be able to help him. First, you will need to notice carefully just which sounds or combinations of sounds are giving him trouble. You might then select some nursery rhymes or songs that feature one or more of the difficult sounds and let him say or sing them with you. For example, the *s* sound is not easy for some young children, but they will not be embarrassed when saying with someone else such rhymes as "Sing a song of sixpence" or "Simple Simon met a pieman," and very likely after some repetitions they will be managing the *s* sounds more correctly, much as a child who cannot carry a tune very well by himself may do better when singing with someone else. If such indirect approaches do not lead to improvement, the parent may even show her child how to hold his lips to make the *s* or other sounds in words that he continues to speak incorrectly. Standing with the child in front of a mirror will help him to imitate with his lips and tongue what you are doing with yours. But try this kind of exercise only if you can make it a kind of play which your child enjoys. Otherwise he may become self-conscious, anxious, or frustrated. If you yourself are overly concerned about your child's incorrect speech, he will sense this and react unfavorably. In such a case, it would probably be better to allow time for his speech to right itself or to find someone to help him who can do so in a cheerful, relaxed manner which he finds agreeable.

The names of numbers can be taught beginning at the three-to-four-year level. Some children may already know "one, two, three," and by five years of age they can usually count to ten or more. Numbers are best taught in relation to objects rather than in the abstract. Children like to learn to count their fingers and toes, the numbers of which incidentally are believed to have initiated our decimal system. At a very early age, the child begins to develop number concepts. He discovers he has two feet and one shoe for each foot, so he has two shoes. He is given a piece of candy which he takes with one hand and then holds out the other hand for another piece. If given several pieces of candy to pass around, one for each person, he may find that there are not quite enough to go around, that one or two members of the family did not get any. You can then let him decide how many more pieces to take, one for this person, and one for the other one who also has none. In learning to set the table, he gradually becomes aware of how many spoons, cups, plates, etc. it takes for all the family. The parents can help their child build into his vocabulary words that he will need in dealing with numerical processes. Consider such everyday remarks as the following: "There were ten cupcakes but now only two are left." "Let's divide up the rest of the pie." "You have one pencil, so why do you want another?" "How many times have I told you to come when I call?" "The wastebaskets are to be emptied twice a week."

By five years of age, your child can learn to recognize written numbers from one to ten, although this may take practice. A simplified game of dominoes, connecting like numbers without adding up the ends of the row, and games like Parcheesi using dice may also be possible for your child at this age if you play them with him in order to give him any help he may need. Watching for numbers he can recognize while riding in the car or on the bus is also fun as are games of counting the number of dogs seen on a walk, the number of people in dark glasses, the number of boys or girls and so on. Also, some nursery rhymes involve numbers, such as "One, two, buckle my shoe;/Three, four, shut the door." And counting is often appropriate when looking at a picture which includes several like items, such as a cat with kittens, or several boys and girls playing a game. Parents who keep in mind how valuable it will be for their child to develop a good number-sense will discover many other informal opportunities to interest him in acquiring the basic concepts and vocabulary he will need to do this.

The language understanding and abilities that your child has when he starts to learn to read serve as the building blocks with which reading is fashioned. To comprehend the meaning of printed material, the child must understand the oral language patterns that the printed words represent, for oral speech precedes and is basic to written language. Reading is responding to talk written down. Once the child understands this, he will have additional motivation to learn to read because he will want to find out what the "talk" says.

Parents must keep in mind that there are individual

differences in language ability at any age. Even so, most children brought up under favorable circumstances will have quite a vocabulary by age two. Many two-year-olds are able to speak about 200 words and understand many more. Estimates suggest that three-year-olds have a vocabulary of about 900 words which increases to about 1,500 by around four years, and up to 3,500 words are mastered by five-year-olds. Whether or not your child is naturally talkative and quick to learn new words and phrases, with your encouragement and guidance he will have made considerable progress in verbal expression by the time he is five years old.

The child who is not inclined to talk very much and is slow to develop the vocabulary he needs to make himself understood can make use of special attention and encouragement from his parents. Marion Monroe in *Growing into Reading* (Scott, Foresman and Co.) has listed the following levels of expressiveness in children's talking: Some children need encouragement to say more than a word or two at a time, while some will make one or two short statements and have no more to say. Others make one or two spontaneous remarks and will add more upon request, while still others talk freely and converse naturally with their parents and friends, whether interpreting a picture, helping with household tasks, or recalling what was seen and done on an excursion.

In planning to help your child become more verbal, you might first consider what level of expressiveness he has already reached, irrespective of his actual age. Perhaps it seems that your three-year-old is slow in talking. Many children do not talk very much until they are between two and three years of age. By about two-and-a-half, most children can carry on a very simple conversation. Usually at that age, a child has acquired a vocabulary which includes some adjectives, such as *big, little, new, hot,* and a few adverbs, such as *fast, too, maybe,* as well as many nouns and a number of verbs, especially those clearly denoting action, such as *come, go, sit* and *play.* Assembling over a period of several days or a week a list of some of the words your three-year-old uses when he does talk may provide some hints as to what kind of help he needs to learn to speak more freely. Does his basic speaking vocabulary seem very limited or does it appear that he knows many words, including the various commonly used parts of speech, but just does not seem interested in combining them? There is also the possibility that he speaks so slowly and hesitantly or is so hard to understand that the listener becomes impatient and either guesses what he is about to say or no longer pays attention. A child will keep trying to express himself only if it seems worthwhile. Why talk when others anticipate your wants and fulfill them or when no one listens? No matter how old the preschool child is who is not as verbal as he should be in order to learn to read and to get along well with adults and other children, there are ways to teach him to express himself more easily, even though it may not be his nature to talk as freely as some other children.

The young child who does not talk readily particularly needs the thoughtful and undivided attention of the parent for at least a short period each day. Especially in a large family, the preschool child may be facing too much competition for a chance to share in conversations. On the other hand, an only child may be so indulged that he seldom needs to ask for anything or to seek approval. As already outlined, the parent can teach the child in the course of shared activities of many kinds. Examining pictures may prove to be especially productive in working with your child who seldom talks spontaneously or elaborates on his initial statement. If he only enumerates the

objects in a picture, you can ask about what the characters are doing: Is the dog walking or running? What is
the girl eating? Once you have reached this stage, questions may lead to interpretation of relationships indicated
in the picture, such as, the dog is running away with the
boy's cap, and the boy is trying to catch him to get the
cap back. The picture may serve as a starting point for
more talk about dogs if your child has a dog or is acquainted with dogs in the neighborhood. Encourage him
to compare the dog in the picture with other dogs he
knows as to color, size, shape of the ears, and so on, helping him as needed with descriptive words and showing
approval of what he says, especially of any attempts at
sentences.

Singing to and with your child will help to increase his
vocabulary and verbal facility. You may think that you
have forgotten songs you knew in your childhood but you
will find you remember an astonishing number of them.
You might also get a book of such songs and learn new
ones. *The Fireside Book of Children's Songs* (Simon and
Schuster) offers a fine collection, and there are many
other such books. Young children particularly like nursery songs and silly songs. They love repetition and will
soon be joining in the singing of all or parts of the song.
And a song often leads to more conversation between
parent and child.

When playing games with the child who is not inclined
to talk, try to carry on a conversation about what is taking
place. Ask your child: "What do you think I am going to
do now? How did you manage to get ahead of me? What
game did you play with Daddy last night and who won?"
Make running comments, such as, "That was a fine play
you made. How stupid of me! Watch out, or I'll get ahead
of you!" Try for spontaneity and fun and in the relaxed,
happy atmosphere your child's enjoyment and excitement

may very well find more expression in speech than is customary for him.

Whenever you can, encourage your child to talk and try to be an interested and sympathetic listener. For instance, when he comes inside after playing out of doors, make a point of talking about what he was doing. The three-year-old may not be able to respond well to the question, "What did you do out in the yard?" but will do better with questions such as "Which truck did you play with in the sandbox?" However he may respond to your interest in what he has been doing while he was playing, be patient with his attempts to talk. And do not criticize the way he says things, for with more practice and experience he will use more precise vocabulary and better grammatical forms. The main thing is to encourage communication. According to Gesell and Ilg in *The Infant and Child in the Culture of Today* (Harper & Row), the three-year-old is beginning to enjoy and use verbal humor. The mother may ask, "Are your socks red today?" and the reply is, "No," with a smile. If mother says, "Then they must be blue." "No, wrong again," laughs the child, showing his white socks.

Four-year-olds are usually ready for more elaborate conversations. Words, such as *different, surprise,* and *guess* which were understood earlier are now likely to be in the speaking vocabulary. The four-year-old will ask "Why?" and "How?" He enjoys new and big words as you introduce them into your conversations with him. Exaggeration appeals to him and he likes to use such expressions as "in a hundred years." Silly talk, such as found in certain nursery tales and songs is also a special delight to children of this age. Also, the four-year-old has become much more social and likes to spend much of his time with other children with whom he talks more and more freely. And he is ready for many excursions to places in the neighborhood and beyond. His widening interests and experience give him more to talk about and add to his vocabulary and understanding. Parents need to be sure to provide him with the opportunities for growth for which he is now ready.

If your child of four still has trouble in verbalizing, he may nonetheless be ready for most of the experiences ordinarily enjoyed at this age. These very experiences, such as trips to places of interest to him and ample opportunity for group play, will provide rich conversational material which the parents can use in drawing him out to talk more freely about what he has seen and done. They can also welcome his questions about whatever is new and strange to him and, instead of just giving quick answers, they can attempt conversations with him about the general subject in which his inquiries indicate he has some interest. Between four and five, your child is ready to listen to longer and less childish stories including humorous ones and these, too, can prompt talking together. At critical points in a story, for example, you can pause and ask, "And what do you suppose happened next?" or "What would you do if something like that happened to you?"

In general, continuing to take ample time to converse with your four-year-old without using any pressure to require him to say more than he is willing and able to do is the best way to help him become more verbal.

Many five-year-olds can carry on a fluent conversation with their playmates or with adults with whom they are well acquainted. From five to six, the child often seems quite grown-up, serious, planful, and practical. He has lost much of his interest in exaggeration and is beginning to distinguish between truth and falsehood. During conversations with your child you can help to clarify this distinction, appreciating his flights of imagination which tend to be brief, but showing how to separate fact from fancy. It is easy to expect too much of a five-year-old, especially if he talks fluently and well. But his view of much of his world is still naive, and he has a limited concept of time and of many other circumstances common to everyday life. On the other hand, if your five-year-old does not express himself well in words, you must guard against treating him as you would a younger child if his main problem is lack of verbal facility.

At the four-year level, it is a good time to teach new vocabulary by arranging situations requiring use of such words as *over, around,* and *through.* With his blocks or toys on the floor, ask your child if he can step *over* them. Then, ask him to walk *around* them, and then *around* a chair and *through* the doorway. Then, to give him practice in using these words correctly, let him have a turn in telling you what to do. On another day, when he has mastered the first set of words, this game can be expanded to include new ones such as *inside, outside, under, above, in front of,* and *behind.* Other variations will help him to increase his store of descriptive words and give him practice in using them. For example, ask him to bring you a small block, then a bigger one, and then the biggest one he has; to reach up high, higher, and the highest he can; to knock softly on the door and then more loudly; or to find some object in the room that is smooth to the touch, another not so smooth, and some other that has a rough surface. The four-year-old will probably need help in learning to get the meaning and use of such comparative words as *many, few* or *none,* and *all, some,* or *several.* Using marbles, beans, buttons, or other small objects such as pebbles, you can devise simple games to acquaint him with words of this sort and provide an enjoyable way for him to practice using them. After your child has mastered new words in games or special exercises, he will like to use them in the course of everyday activities if you will watch for and alert him to opportunities to do so.

Most parents engage in some of the activities with their preschool child as outlined in this chapter. But too many do so in a somewhat haphazard way without realizing their importance in developing their child's verbal facility. With more understanding of the ways in which a child's speech development can be fostered, parents can select and time their efforts with greater precision and effectiveness. By so doing, they can planfully prepare their child for the complex task of learning to read.

Chapter 7.
Your Child Learns to Listen

Learning to read depends to a large degree upon good listening habits. The reader must become familiar with many sound patterns as indicated in print and be able to make such fine distintcions as the difference in the middle sounds of *horse* and *house* or *shall* and *shell.* Otherwise he cannot pronounce or comprehend what he is trying to read. Learning to hear word sounds involves paying attention to loudness or intensity, to pitch, to tone quality, and sometimes to duration. Without any consciously directed home-training, many children by the time they enter school will have gained considerable skill in distinguishing between sound patterns. But, with a moderate amount of help from their parents, many others also could have learned to do this. Every preschool child could benefit from some guidance in learning to listen to words with discrimination.

The young child is surrounded by sounds of many kinds, such as the footsteps of his parents, the noise of a passing car, raindrops on the roof, the wind blowing, a door banging, a faucet dripping, a dog barking, the TV and radio playing. He also hears people both speak and sing. What can he do about all the sounds he hears? He can ignore a sound or listen to it and try to imitate it, or listen and associate meaning with the sound. Oral speech is based upon imitation of heard talk. In fact, the child who cannot hear cannot learn to talk intelligibly without highly specialized training. The meaning a child associates with a sound is derived from his experience. The noise of a vacuum cleaner will be startling, and perhaps even frightening, to the young child until he learns that it is only cleaning the floors and carpets. The sounds of his mother's voice, at first merely pleasurable, gradually takes on meanings which he understands and begins to imitate, as he does with the other voices he hears. Eventually he develops the ability to express himself verbally.

Sounds differ in several ways. They may be so soft that they can hardly be heard or so loud as to be disagreeable. It is easiest to listen to a voice that has a median, comfortable intensity, for it is easily heard yet not unpleasantly loud. Sounds also vary in pitch. The squeaking of mice and the chirping and songs of some birds are high pitched. And the sound of a river or harbor boat whistle, or of a truck rumbling by, is low pitched. All musical instruments have a range of notes from low to high pitch, as does the human voice. The tone quality, or timbre, of the same pitched tone varies with different instruments. The variation in tone quality is due to the number and intensity of the different vibration frequencies in a tone.

Voices of people vary in intensity, pitch, and tone quality. Extremes in either intensity or pitch are not as pleasing as the middle ranges. Richness of tone quality due to the presence of several vibrating frequencies in the tone is ordinarily pleasant. The duration of sounds in speech also contributes to ease of understanding what is said. Successive speech sounds in words and sentences can be too fast or too slow for good understanding. Particularly with young children, the parent should speak at a somewhat slower rate than is customary in adult communication.

Training in hearing involves paying attention to loudness or intensity, pitch, tone quality, and sometimes to duration of sounds. Even before your child can talk, you can help him learn to identify sounds that alert him. For example, be sure that he not only hears but also sees the dog barking, watches the washing machine and the vacuum cleaner in operation, and has toys with bells or that readily make other sounds. When he is older and is talking, you can teach him words to describe sounds he hears, such as *rattle, bang, hiss, roar, rumble, whistle, tick, tinkle,* and *squeak,* and encourage him to tell you what he hears and to name or look for its source. He will learn to distinguish between the ordinary horn of an automobile and the fire or ambulance siren, a fly buzzing and the purr of a cat, and the sound of rain on the roof and that of a shower.

Without guidance in paying attention to sounds, describing them, and noting their source, many children learn very little even about those sounds they hear most frequently. Only those sounds that they know and like and occasional strange and startling sounds tend to command their attention. And it may not occur to them to try to describe, compare, and attempt to analyze even familiar sounds, such as the bark of the dog and the meow of the cat. Some sounds, when identified, such as the hum or roar of traffic on a nearby street, are best ignored. But other sounds require attentive listening, as the parent telling his child where to find his shoes. To say to your child, "Pay attention," usually means stop listening to something else and listen to me. Thus a child often needs to stop listening to something of interest in order to respond to a call to dinner or directions to start getting ready for bed.

There are many ways in which parents can teach their child to listen with discrimination. For example, call attention to the chirping of a cricket, noting the characteristic high pitch which can be interesting to anyone, especially a child. Differences in pitch often occur in reading a story to a child. A good example is the story of The Three Bears. The fun of listening is largely due to the differences in the pitch of voice of Father Bear, Mother Bear, and Baby Bear. If the parent uses the terms "low" and "high" in referring to the voices of Father Bear

and Baby Bear, this will aid in directing the child to differences in pitch.

To teach your child to discriminate duration and sequence of sounds, shake a rattle or ring a bell for a few
seconds and then drop an object, such as a spoon, on the
table. Point out to him that the first sound is longer and
the second one shorter. Let him practice doing this. Again,
have him run fast while you tap rapidly on the table, and
then walk slowly while you tap slowly. Point out the
difference by using the terms "fast" and "slow" and have
him use them and demonstrate. Help him from then on
in the course of his daily activities to find many situations
in which he can practice noting and talking about sounds
that are longer or shorter, faster or slower, and which
comes first or second, until he can make relatively fine
discriminations as to their duration and sequence.

You can then use nursery rhymes ot teach the duration
of sounds in language. For instance, take the lines:

> Hickory, dickory dock,
> The mouse ran up the clock.

Let your child repeat after you the two lines and, if necessary, practice them until he speaks them easily, clearly,
and correctly. Then ask him which word took the longest
to say, *hickory* or *dock*. You can vary the question by using
some of the other words, such as *dickory* and *mouse* or
clock. If he has trouble at first in determining which of
two words takes longer to say, ask him to listen carefully
while you say them and exaggerate the difference somewhat. Then, let him repeat them. When he can answer
correctly without your help, you will know that he can
distinguish the difference in duration of the words in the
pairs you have given him. Similar games can be played
with other nursery rhymes or jingles, such as "Here we
go round the mulberry bush" or "Hickety, pickety, my

black hen." Rhymes are better than just any words for these beginning exercises because the beat of the rhythm accents the duration of the words.

Auditory discrimination of the many different sounds in words is very important as a basis for reading. Hearing skills ordinarily develop slowly as the child is growing up from two to six. They will develop more rapidly with some help from parents. Most children at quite an early age are capable of noting that certain words begin with the same sound: *doll, dog, dig, down,* etc. You can play a game with your child, helping him to think up words that all begin with the same sound as a word you choose or he chooses. Whenever, in the course of the game, he names a word that does not begin with the right sound, demonstrate to him the difference. By the time your child is four or five years old, probably he will also be able to note that certain words end with the same sound: *bell, tell, sell, well,* etc. Again, a game can be played by starting him off with a word such as *man* and asking him to think of other words that end with the same sound. Other starting words might be: *red* or *book* or *ball.*

Remember that the spelling of a word does not matter in these games, only the sounds. *Jam* and *gym* begin with the same sound and *you* and *zoo* end in the same sound, although spelled quite differently.

From a very early age, your child has probably had experience in listening to nursery rhymes and jingles. In all this, he has become somewhat aware of rhyming words and probably has begun to distinguish some of them. A good way to increase his understanding of rhymes is as follows: First, call his attention to words that sound alike in some rhymes he knows, such as Jack and *Jill* went up the *hill,* pointing out that *Jill* sounds like *hill.* Then, choose another line of some nursery rhyme familiar to him and ask him to give the last word of the two that rhyme, such as Little Jack Horner sat in a _____. When he supplies *corner,* make sure that he recognizes that it rhymes with *Horner*. Do similar things with other rhymes, such as *See-saw*, Margery *Daw*. A book of "Mother Goose" or some other one that offers a good selection of nursery rhymes will be useful in continuing this game. Include some verses that have the rhyming word at the end of the second line, such as:

> Humpty Dumpty sat on a *wall,*
> Humpty Dumpty had a great *fall.*

Your child will like this game and at the same time gain in sensitivity of sound discrimination. Play this game on different days, not continuing it long enough at any one time for it to bore your child. This suggestion applies to all such games or other learning activities because zest for what he is doing is what promotes learning from doing it. A child's attention span tends to increase year by year, but there are always individual differences. When your child's attention begins to wander, it is time to stop the game for the time being.

When your child does pretty well in detecting and naming the rhyming words in several nursery rhymes, a next step is to see if he can think of other words that rhyme with words in the verse, such as with *pie* and *cry* in "Georgie Porgie, pudding and *pie,*/Kissed the girls and made them *cry*." Suggest one or two, such as *my* and *fly*, and your child may be able to think of others, such as *sky, why, try, fry*. Another example suitable for the beginner might be *Jill* and *hill* in "Jack and *Jill* went up the *hill*/To fetch a pail of water," as many words known to the child end in "ill," such as *fill, mill, bill, still*.

With a little help and encouragement, many children will soon be able to make their own jingles with rhyming words. When suggesting that your child try this, give an example, such as "I *wish* I had a *fish*" or "The little white *cat* ran after the *rat*," calling attention to the words that rhyme. At first he may not quite get the idea and think only of rhymes he remembers from ones you have told him or read to him from one of his books. In any case, give enthusiastic approval of his effort.

Another word game that is something like a riddle calls attention to similar but different sounds in words. Take two words that sound somewhat alike, such as *picture* and *pitcher,* and ask "Does that book have *pitchers* in it or *pictures*?" Or, "What do we buy candy with, *money* or *monkey*?" You will think up other such pairs of words, such as, "What do you sit on, a *chair* or a *cheer*?" And, "Which can we ride on, a *pony* or a *penny*?" Or, "Which do we wear when it is cold, *kittens* or *mittens*?" The nonsense element in this game makes it great fun, and your child will be learning to listen carefully to give the right answer. Here are a few additional pairs of words suitable for use in this game: *play* and *pray*; *sheep* and *sheet*; *boot* and *boat*; *bread* and *bed*; *glass* and *grass*; *sandwich* and *sandbox*; *seashell* and *seesaw*; *ship* and *shop*; *child* and *chilled*; *bottle* and *bubble*.

Children love alliteration, such as found in many nursery rhymes that feature two or three words all starting with the same sound, or like sounds: Bye, baby bunting; My maid Mary; A Dillar, a dollar; Goosey, goosey, gander. After a little practice in thinking of words that begin with the same sound, such as *bell* and *ball*, a game may be devised of finding alliterative titles to pictures in old magazines, such as, A Baby in a Bed, A Train on Tracks, A Cow and a Calf, A Boy and a Ball. If this chances to be too difficult, you can help the child by pointing out some possibilities by asking, "How about this one and that one?" Then, let him cut out the picture for which he finds a alliterative title. Such pictures can be accumulated and used over and over again. An inexpensive picture dictionary is a good source for finding pictures that start with the same sound as the words.

Many of these word games are useful when children get restless on a long drive or while waiting in the car, especially when the game chosen is already familiar to the child. They can also be played with the child while his mother is ironing or otherwise occupied with household tasks not requiring her undivided attention. Without a moderate amount of such consciously directed home-training, many children will have difficulty in distinguishing some of the likenesses and differences in word sounds they will need to recognize when beginning to read. The child who, upon entering first grade, can already make such fine distinctions as the difference between *horse* and *house* or *shall* and *shell,* where attention must be given to the middle sound of the word, as well as discriminate the beginning and ending sounds, such as in *fan* and *fat* or *man* and *pan,* will be off to a fine start in learning to read. It has been found that the child of four and five has less trouble in learning to discriminate word sounds if the words are in phrases or sentences rather than in meaningless sequence. For this reason, using rhymes as suggested above is a good exercise. In all the games with words, clear and precise enunciation in speech patterns should be encouraged. The child who habitually says "git" for "get" will have trouble with that word when he encounters it in print, or if he says "hafta" for "have to," both the correct pronunciation and the meaning may escape him when he is trying to read those words in his primer. After your child begins to read, the teacher will introduce further training in auditory discrimination as needed. Thus, as the school year progresses, readiness instruction will merge with systematic reading instruction.

In developing auditory skills, it should be emphasized that words are pronounced as units. When words are spoken this way, the child will learn to hear within the whole auditory pattern the beginning, the ending, and less often the middle, sounds in each word. With some words it is rather difficult to discriminate the middle sound, as in *house* and *horse*. But with others it is much easier, as in *tall* and *tell*. The parent should be careful not to break up a word into the different sounds in beginning and middle and end in trying to acquaint his child with it. Sometimes it is desirable to speak a word slowly for the child, that is to drawl the sounds out without any break between them. This will help him to attend to the successive sounds, yet still hear the word as a whole.

With some help from their parents, all children can learn to listen to and discriminate between many sounds before entering school. This will do much to remove a common stumbling block in learning to read. Quite early, all children will learn without any special help to discriminate between common sounds around the house, in the yard, and on the street. Also, a child will learn to distinguish one word from another. But it is sounds within words to which he must attend when he is learning to read. Ordinarily, he does not learn to do this without help. Informal individual teaching at home during the years four and five is better suited to the needs of the child in developing his ability to distinguish word sounds than group instruction after he enters school. As outlined in this chapter, such teaching can best be accomplished through games and play. As the preschool child's attention span tends to be rather short, these activities should not last long at any one time. It is better to stop as soon, or even before, your child becomes restless or inattentive. Some of the games present him with brand new concepts and tax his ability to grasp what it is all about, however simple they may seem to grown-ups who cannot even remember when they could not readily distinguish word sounds. So, when dealing with beginning, middle, or ending sounds of words, use only three or four examples at a time.

Learning to listen attentively and well to all sorts of sounds, to identify them, and to concentrate on those which are judged significant is a necessary and often a gratifying and productive part of living. Parents can do much to alert their very young child to sounds that will be of interest to him and to develop his ability to distinguish them. From around four years of age until he enters the first grade, helping him to note and recognize sounds within words and to enunciate them correctly will provide a valuable part of his preparation for the difficult task of learning to read.

Chapter 8.
Children Use Their Eyes

Adjustment of the eyes for reading words in a sentence is a highly complex activity. The preschool child can learn a great deal about how to use his eyes for effective seeing and so become prepared for the task of vision in reading. While in the natural course of growth and development a child makes considerable gains in his ability to make correct visual observations, his parents can aid him to do so with increasing skill.

Children begin to distinguish objects with their eyes at a very early age, and this ability develops month by month and year by year. By one year of age, a child can coordinate vision in his two eyes sufficiently to pick up small objects. As he progresses from one to two years, this two-eyed (binocular) vision improves. But at eighteen months of age your child still has very little perception of far-off objects. As he begins his second year, his eye-hand coordination improves rapidly. He enjoys piling one block upon another—but with little regard to their size— and putting them into a toy wagon or pail and then dumping them out. He will manipulate clay, likes to dabble with finger paints and play with pots and pans. His favorite toys are apt to be ones he can pull around or hammer. And by eighteen months or so, his growing eye-hand coordination and improved sense of balance enables him to climb up on furniture or outdoor play equipment, which he dearly loves to do even before he is quite equal to it. At around two years of age, your child will notice and recognize clear pictures of familiar objects in his picture books, and before he is three he will turn the pages of a book but not necessarily one at a time.

During the three-year period, your child's ability to coordinate his eyes and his hands will increase so much that he will enjoy concentrating for lengthening periods of time on one project and take pride in the results. He can string large beads on a cord, carry silverware to and from the table, use crayons and a coloring book with increasing success, undress himself with little or no help, and handle his spoon and his cup with much less spilling. He chooses and balances his blocks with more skill and shapes clay into a rope, a ball, or a pancake, as he may decide. His painting and drawing begin to show signs of design, and he handles brush and crayon in a more adult manner. He is ready to learn to ride a tricycle but may only push it around for a while. He is becoming much better able to handle himself on play equipment in the yard or at the playground, but he still needs watching. Picture books now delight him and, as he explores details in a picture, he may try to explain what he sees.

As your child moves on through the fourth year and into the fifth, he continues to gain precision in the accurate use of his eyes and in the control of his hand and other bodily movements. He has become agile in the use of his wrists and fingers for finer manipulation of objects instead of using the whole arm as he did at an earlier age. Although his drawings have become more elaborate and include recognizable designs and even crude letters, he still gives little attention to size or space relationships. Details he considers most important are usually drawn largest. Books and pictures are becoming much more interesting to him. He will sit by himself enjoying the pictures and will now turn the pages expertly. He often knows which book to get for a favorite story he wants read to him and may recognize and like to pick out certain letters he can name correctly. These letters he may have learned in viewing alphabet books as you have read the text to him. Probably he is learning to recognize some printed numbers and can begin to distinguish the big and little hands of the clock and see what numbers they are on. He can now dress himself with little or no help and do various simple household tasks and errands and recall details of what he has seen on trips taken away from home some days or weeks in the past. His constructions with blocks have become quite complicated and he can put a jigsaw puzzle together if it has fairly large pieces.

Your five-year-old is ready for kindergarten experiences. These will be considered in detail in Chapters 11 and 12. He is growing up fast and already exercises rather accurate visual control of most of his activities. And he is now ready for additional visual experiences that will further prepare him for beginning reading. While parents are well aware of the lack of eye-hand coordination of the very young child, by the age of five and later, his visual control has become so much more precise that it is frequently taken for granted. But, without guidance and ample opportunities to exercise his visual control in an ever-widening range of activities, your child will miss much that is important. Let us now consider in what ways parents can foster visual efficiency in their child.

At around six months of age, your child needs a few safe objects to play with. Usually he will be interested in only one toy at a time but will tire of it and then like another which he will grasp, bang around, drop, and then try to pick up. He may look directly at his rattle or soft toy that lies within his reach, but his hands may not be deft enough to pick it up even after several attempts. But eye-hand coordination is getting underway. For a good share of his waking hours, he needs to be where he can watch household activity and make whatever response he chooses when spoken to. He may just look toward the voice and smile or may wave his arms and make sounds. In any case, he is getting necessary practice in seeing and hearing whatever is going on and in making eye movements and focusing.

From one to two, your child will prefer several toys at

a time and will pick one up, look at it, shake it or bang it, drop it, and then pick up another. Now he will try to roll a ball back that is rolled to him and likes such shared activity, watching attentively what you do and making somewhat related responses. At fifteen or eighteen months, try placing a block or a spoon in front of him within easy reach of his arm. He will use a grasping movement of his arm and hand to pick it up and will probably succeed. After he has examined it, place it a little to one side of him, then a little nearer or farther away to give him practice in reaching it from different angles. At around two years of age, your child's wrists and fingers have become agile enough for him to change objects from one hand to another and to manage other finer manipulations. Present him with a small pail and give him a little guidance in filling it with blocks and then dumping them out. He still likes pull toys but is becoming more interested in toys with parts that he can directly manipulate, such as wheels to turn or buttons to push or balls that he can hammer through holes into their box. Although the two-year-old is ready for many constructive activities and to observe and learn many things, he cannot be left long to his own devices, or his behavior is apt to become disorganized and destructive. Parents need to spend a great deal of time with their two-year-old, helping with and watching over his attempts at eye-hand coordination, seeing that he has appropriate play materials, taking him on short walks and helping him to see and identify whatever will interest him, familiarizing him with nursery rhymes and songs, providing him with practice in looking at pictures and naming objects in them, and letting him not only watch but also take some small part in various household tasks.

Many activities first undertaken during the second year are continued on an ever-advancing level throughout the third year and beyond, with new interests added from time to time. With the beginning of the fourth year, the child has become much more self-sufficient and now requires less constant supervision. His play is more organized, and he listens longer to stories read to him. The parents should take advantage of their child's lengthened span of attention by spending longer periods with him in reading and telling stories, singing and listening to children's records, and examining pictures in more detail. Some time-honored games, such as hide-the-thimble (or some other small object), hide-and-seek, or hunting peanuts in their shells hidden around the house are fun for children of this age and require thorough searching and "sharp eyes." The three-year-old is also ready for more extended walks and trips to watch men at a construction site or repairing a street, or to look at all the different foods in the market.

While children of three and four are not old enough to easily note similarities between objects, they are beginning to be conscious of differences and can be aided by their parents to be more observing and discriminating. It is not too soon to begin to teach your child to recognize the basic or fundamental colors: red, green, yellow, blue, black, and white. At first, show solid-colored objects of each of these six colors, such as a red apple or ball, a yellow lemon or piece of paper, a white cup or bowl, a green leaf or lime, a blue box or dish. Ask your child if he knows the color of one of the objects and help with the name if necessary. Suggest that he look around to see if he can see another object of that same color and ask if he can remember ever having seen an object of that color. Practice with only one or two new colors a day. Between times, use color designations whenever appropriate in talking with your child, as "Here is your blue shirt" or "Look how green the grass is." Threading colored beads is a good way to give practice in observing and naming colors. Ask your child what color is the last bead he has put on and what color he is going to use next. Do not try to teach the intermediate colors until your child is at least five years old, that is, colors such as purple, orange, or pink. After your three- or four-year-old knows some of the colors, he will like to practice them when you and he walk around the neighborhood. See what fundamental colors there are that he knows in foliage, flowers, buildings, signs, and cars parked along the street, and give him help if he needs it in identifying them. Encourage some conversation about the color of each object examined. Soon your child will be talking spontaneously about colors as he sees or recalls them. A few boys are color-blind. This will show up when such a boy persistently confuses reds and greens or shows no interest in the color games mentioned above.

Parents can teach quite a young child to discriminate between sizes and shapes of objects long before he would be likely to do so without any help. Starting with sizes, it will be well at first to compare only two objects at a time. Show your child a broom and a whisk broom, and ask him to point out any difference. If he says that this one is small and that one is big, ask him another time which is smaller and which is bigger and have him reply, using those words to better prepare him to verbalize such comparisons. After whatever practice seems indicated with similar pairs of objects of differing sizes around the house, you can present three such objects at a time for him to designate as small, smaller, smallest, or big, bigger, biggest. Then he will probably be ready to work with a series of objects, such as blocks or dishes of different sizes, arranging them in order of size, either in a pile starting with the biggest or in a row. Encourage him to tell you what he is doing and how he is doing it, so that he will be getting practice in putting into words what his eyes and hands are doing. Pictures of objects of different sizes found in magazines or picture books will offer your child a chance to make still finer discriminations between big and small.

Teach your child to recognize and distinguish between a few common shapes and their various forms. Very likely he already knows that a ball is round. Explain to him that a circle is round, too, but also flat. Let him look around for other round objects and decide whether they are round like a ball, flat like the paper circle, or appear in some other forms, such as the top and bottom of a cup. Show him how to make a paper chain or necklace by using strips of paper and Scotch tape to make interlocking rings. In a similar manner, give your child experience in viewing and naming square objects, such as a square box or block and square pieces of paper. For a while, do not expect him to make fine discriminations between squares and rectangles. For providing experience with other shapes, see Chapter 6. When he has become somewhat acquainted with words to use in designating and describing shapes, watch for opportunities for him to use them in the course of daily activities so that they will become firmly fixed in his vocabulary.

Exercises outlined above and others of a similar nature will accustom your child to make careful visual discrimination of the details of objects and pictures. Also, he will be developing a greater ability in giving clear verbal expression of what he sees. He is taking steps toward making the finer visual discriminations that will be required in recognizing letters in words. A further step in this direction can be taken by learning to note and compare internal details of objects and pictures, much as he will need to do later with letters within printed words. Many objects are quite similar except for a slight difference in some detail which a child may not note at first glance. For instance, two cats may be about the same size and color except that one has a white spot on its face or on one foot. Or two cars may resemble each other in just about all respects except that one is a two-door and the other has four doors. Two dishes may be identical except for a small nick on the edge of one of them. You will not find it difficult to interest your child in trying to discover and talk with you about such differences which at first are not apparent to him.

Television is another medium which, when used with discretion, will help your child develop his ability to make visual discriminations. *Sesame Street* has many exercises in distinguishing visually and expressing verbally the differences in many of the details of the situations represented. Other programs of interest to your child will serve the same purpose to some extent. It is desirable for the parent to select the television pictures to be watched by the preschool child and, whenever possible, to watch it with him, calling attention now and then to details he might otherwise miss and explaining whatever may puzzle or confuse him. When you see a program together, you can talk it over and refer to it afterward.

Developing the concepts of left and right and moving from left to right are necessary in learning to read. With guidance, the preschool child can be prepared to do this. A first step is to teach your child to know which is his right and which is his left hand. For a beginning, tie a loose string around his wrists, explaining to him it is his right hand that has a string around it. Point out that people always shake hands with their right hands and practice this with him. Also, play a game of "Simon says, raise your right hand; raise your left hand; put your right hand here; put your left hand there"; and so on, varying the procedure to keep it interesting. You might then set two cups on the table, one with the handle on his left and the other with the handle on his right. Vary this until he has little or no difficulty in telling which handle is on his right or left or until he becomes tired of the game for the time being. When riding in the car, call your child's attention to the right and left sides of the road and teach him to notice whether you are making a left or a right turn. When looking at pictures together, you will find many opportunities to have him make further use of the terms "left" and "right." After pointing out to him the right-hand page and the left-hand page, you can have him turn the right-hand page to see a new picture or turn back the left-hand page to see again a picture you have already seen. Within the picture, some left and right positions may be noted. With a little help, your child may determine, for example, that "the boy is building a tower on the left side of the fireplace." Descriptions of exercises to teach other positions such as "above," "below," "between" are given in Chapter 6.

Reading English and many other languages requires movement of the eyes from left to right along a line of print. Some preliminary practice in proceeding in the left-to-right direction can be given to preschool children. The sequence of action pictures for children progresses from left to right. Comics that are read to your child are also arranged this way. As you read the comic sequence, point to the first picture on the left, as you read the print connected with it. Then, continue to point to each picture, as you proceed to the right. After a while, your child can do the pointing. To further demonstrate moving from left to right, draw a picture of a cat on the left side of a sheet of paper and a dish of food on the right side, and then raise the question, "Toward what direction will the cat go to get his food?" Whether he draws his finger across the paper or replies verbally, say, "Yes he will go toward the right." Then, let him draw a line with a crayon to show

how the cat moves from left to right to get his food. You can readily devise other similar situations. At the preschool age it is better not to work with lines of print since these can have little meaning before the child has begun to learn to read. All that is necessary before going to school is developing the habit of looking at pictures from left to right because this will initiate the left-to-right eye movements which will make it easier for your child when he begins to learn to read.

Children will enjoy these visual-discrimination exercises if they are presented as part of their play activities rather than as a required drill. Care must be exercised to keep the activity within the ability of the child in order to experience success. Be generous with your approval of success. If there is failure, try to find the difficulty and simplify the task where indicated. Success with approval brings self-satisfaction and eagerness for further experiences.

Visual difficulties interfere with clear vision even at the preschool age. There are certain observations that the parent can make that may indicate some visual deficiency that needs medical attention. Your child's eyes are in constant use during his waking hours for general viewing of objects near and far and for finer discrimination of certain details close at hand. Symptoms of visual difficulty which the parents may note in their child include: inflammation of the eyes, complaints of headache, habitual tilting of the head when examining pictures or objects, squinting with obvious tension and strain when examining pictures and objects, and crossed eyes or eyes that turn outward. When your child, ages three and above, has any of these symptoms, you should have his eyes checked by an eye specialist. If a difficulty requiring attention is discovered, it should be corrected promptly, if that is possible.

As your child reaches the age of five to six he should

be learning to recognize the letters of the alphabet and the symbols used for numbers. Also, he can be learning to distinguish between some words as the same or different. This will be discussed in Chapters 11 and 12.

The visual skills of children in school depend heavily upon whatever experiences they have had during their preschool years. With adequate exposure to situations and exercises as described above, your child can be expected to learn to use careful visual examination of the details of whatever captures his attention. Without some help from his parents in developing his capacities for visual discrimination during the early years, a child may arrive at kindergarten accustomed to note only gross visual differences in whatever he looks at. But with some care on your part in providing play activities and exercises in the form of play, your child will have developed the ability to discriminate among small details and to attend to close visual tasks such as will confront him in learning to read. Adequate visual discrimination along with auditory discrimination—described in Chapter 7—*are fundamental skills in beginning reading, as well as later on. Without such skills, your child will not be ready for reading but will have to acquire them after entering school, thus postponing his reading instruction.*

Chapter 9.
Physical Development and the Maturation of Abilities

Every child develops physically, mentally, and emotionally from birth onward throughout the preschool period and later, at his own rate. By the time a child is eighteen months to two years of age, his characteristic behavior and individual personality traits are becoming more recognizable. Each child differs in countless ways from all other children. Parents are uniquely situated to watch over the growth and development of their child, to observe his traits and abilities at successive age periods, and during the preschool years to initiate his education. To do this effectively they need to be familiar with the basic trends of growth common to all children and to learn to take into account the ways in which their own child differs from others. Only then can they hope to tailor their teaching and guidance to fully meet his developing needs. The child whose parents have managed to provide him with whatever variety of experience he has been ready for from infancy on, with due regard for the rate and manner of his growth, will be well prepared to enjoy school and to learn to read when he enters the first grade.

Even before learning to talk, the very young child has made strides in motor development. By one year of age, he has acquired overall motor control sufficient for crawling, creeping, or moving about in one way or another, pulling himself to a standing position, picking up and putting down or throwing certain objects, holding a cup and drinking from it, and so on. Following are some of the motor skills your child will be acquiring and perfecting during the next few years, with suggestions regarding your role in observing and helping him. From your observations you will acquire a general idea of the range and limitations of your child's motor behavior at any given period and therefore will be better able to guide him in his activities.

When he is about two years old, note the kinds and degree of your child's overall motor activity as related to his finer coordinations in such activities as walking, running, and climbing. How steady is he on his feet when walking on floors, the lawn, and on uneven ground? Can he climb stairs? The two-year-old usually does not alternate his feet in doing this. Probably he cannot yet balance himself on one foot. In running, you will note that he leans forward more than an older child does. You can also note what finer hand skills are developing as he plays with his toys, uses a paint brush or does finger painting, takes off and helps put on his clothes, and feeds himself. He can now use one hand or the other more freely, turn door knobs that he can reach or wheels on his toys, handle his spoon more adeptly with greater wrist action, and he may be able to hold his cup with one hand. Some children at this age are still very messy while eating; others are not. The two-year-old can usually turn pages of a book but not always one at a time.

As your child approaches three, he is on the threshold of much more controlled activity which will soon develop. But for the time being, he may seem unpredictable, contrary, and not inclined to continue any activity however interested he seemed to be in it when he started. He is making a transition from the relatively stable two-year level to the much better organized three-year period. For the time being, he lacks self-control sufficient to handle and direct his rapidly developing motor drives and, though now becoming aware of alternatives, cannot readily choose between them. He demands something, such as a favorite food, only to push it away, or he clings to some object, refusing to give it up, and then drops it instead of playing with it. But he is making gains in many motor skills. If you will note his drawing, painting, and play with blocks, or with sand, mud, or clay, you will probably see that he is beginning to show interest in form and now has the motor control to give this interest some expression. The lines he draws no longer appear so aimless but often have a direction, either vertical, horizontal, or curved; his block structures begin to be somewhat symmetrical; and he shapes sand or mud into balls or ropes or other forms to which he assigns meaning. However, this purposeful play is apt to occur in spurts to be followed by much less controlled behavior.

When he is three years old, you will find that your child is becoming much more stable and self-directed in the use of his motor skills which are definitely increasing. He walks more like an adult, and is more sure and nimble on his feet, and can use them alternately in going up and down stairs. Given the opportunity, he will probably walk, run, and jump in fairly good time to music. To movements of the whole hand, he now adds selective use of fingers, as in making holes in clay or little tunnels in sand. His drawings, coloring, and use of sand, clay, and blocks are showing more variation and complexity in form and purpose even though the results may be readily recognizable only to himself.

From four to five another transition is underway from the rather calm, satisfying achievements of three to the much higher level of motor performance characteristic of the five-year-old. You will probably find the motor activity of your child between four and five somewhat hard to live with as compared to that of the year before when he was usually cooperative and seemed content with all his newly acquired interests and skills. Do not be surprised if your four-year-old seems overactive and sometimes heedless as he races about on foot, up and down stairs or around the yard on his tricycle, or he darts off on his own when you take him for a walk. Also, you may find him shoving the furniture around to arrange some structure for his imaginative play. If you will accept all this motor drive and increasing but imperfected skills as a natural part of the growth process, you will usually be able to direct them into proper channels. He is ready for excursions beyond house and yard, needs well-chosen play equipment, and can become interested in helping you around the house. He is also ready and eager for group play which, however, will require quite a bit of adult supervision. Frequent trips to the park are now in order to use the trapeze and other play equipment, as are simple singing games, block constructions with other children, and somewhat longer periods of painting and drawing during which he will need rather large supplies of paper and coloring materials. You will note that your four-year-old holds brush or crayon in about the same way as an adult. He and his playmates may now construct complicated patterns with their blocks, such as tracks for their trains to which they add switches, spur tracks, underpasses, bridges, and stations, or making elaborate houses or playgrounds for their dolls. There are many household tasks requiring quite a bit of motor skill in which your child can now participate, such as preparing the table for a meal and clearing up afterward, making his bed, packing away toys in their boxes, and running simple errands. If he has been encouraged to do so, very likely he can now dress himself, as he has learned to tell front from back, and his finger control now permits learning to put buttons into their holes successfully, as well as to handle zippers properly.

The year from five to six resembles in some ways that from three to four in that most children at this level are consolidating gains rather than forging ahead. Your five-year-old will probably be at ease with himself much of the time and usually comfortable with others. His motor skills have become adequate for most of the activities that especially interest him and include considerable control of both overall and finer coordinations. If his motor development has proceeded according to normal expectations, he is ready for the activities of kindergarten which will serve to supplement continuing growth experiences at home.

The parents who carefully observe their child as he progresses through the stages of motor development outlined above and guide him into activities as he becomes able to manage them with satisfaction and pride are enabling him to develop and mature at his maximum rate.

It is well established that a child's ability to learn to read is dependent upon his oral language. Parents will do well to observe and guide their child's language development. In some respects this is more difficult to do well than to observe and provide for his growth in motor skills as discussed above. Vocabulary and speech patterns reflect the specific environment provided for the child and also his individual personality and the ways in which his perceptions and ideas develop. It is generally known that all children make many vocal sounds before forming them into words, that they use nouns and a few common verbs of action before other parts of speech and phrases before sentences, and that their understanding of what is said to them always exceeds their ability to express themselves verbally. But the development of language occurs at less precise age levels than the acquisition of motor abilities.

Your child will probably say his first words at around one year of age, though perhaps a month or so earlier and very possibly not until fifteen months, or even later. Progress in talking tends to be slow at first and then more rapid. During this early period of limited verbal expression, you can be gaining some practice in observing your child's use of words and his understanding of what he hears others say. To watch and guide his speech development will require much thoughtful listening on your part throughout the preschool years and beyond. Only then will you learn how best to communicate with him and to encourage him to speak more freely and adequately.

When your child has become accustomed to naming what he sees in a picture, you may find it helpful in studying his language patterns to initiate the following exercise, which then can be repeated or more or less duplicated from time to time as his ability to express himself verbally increases. Carefully select a picture you know will interest him that depicts two persons or a person and an animal engaged in some action he will have no trouble in identifying. Place the picture before him and ask him to tell you about it. Whatever he may note first in the picture, encourage him by saying, "That's fine. Tell me about what else you see." It will be well to write down everything he says so that you can examine it later. You may elicit additional responses by asking a few questions about the objects he names to determine whether or not he is yet inclined to talk more about what he sees and whether he is able to do so. Perhaps he can tell you what the boy is doing or where the bird is sitting or whether the little girl is walking or running, but perhaps he is only in the stage of naming the objects he sees.

Later stages in a child's language development can be illustrated in relation to a picture of a little girl and a dog that is running with a doll in its mouth. If, when you show your child this picture, his response is merely, "It's a girl and a dog," he appears to be concerned only with things as separate items. Possibly he would say more if he were better able to put his observations and thoughts into words. As his language and thought mature, his responses to such a picture will be made at progressively higher levels, as: "The dog is running away with the girl's doll"; "The girl is unhappy and is crying because the dog took her doll and is running away with it"; "The girl is all upset because the dog has her doll. She is frightened. She does not know how to get the doll back. She wants someone to come and help her"; "He is a bad dog. He does not know that the girl feels hurt and is crying. He does not know how much little girls love their dolls. Dogs should be better trained if they are going to play with children." You will note that in this illustration the gradation of responses ranges from the naming of objects, to their interaction, to their probable feelings and thoughts, to need for outside help in resolving the problem situation, to the opinions of the viewer about it all.

By the use of this type of exercise with your child from time to time and jotting down his responses, you can observe and analyze his progress in verbal facility. This will guide you in structuring your conversations with him. Keeping in mind that his verbal output usually falls somewhat short of the level of his thoughts, you can test out how much he is able to understand when you talk to him on a level somewhat higher than the one from which he responds. The parent should not talk down to his child, but neither should he expect the child to understand what is not yet within his capacity. Your child will tend to imitate your speech and needs ample opportunity to increase his verbal facility through enjoyable and challenging conversations with you. You may know that he has many more ideas than he can clearly express. Then you can help him enlarge his vocabulary and practice saying the same thing in different ways. Or perhaps your child is a chatterbox but does not have many ideas to express. Such a child is apt to have difficulty in claiming the attention he seeks. Parents, becoming bored, may tell him to keep quiet for a while or to run and play. But verbal facility is too important to be discouraged. While remembering that individuals differ throughout life in their talkativeness, you can do much to develop whatever capacity your child may have to express himself verbally in ways that will gain favorable responses and bring him satisfaction.

To help your child who chatters to become more thoughtful and to react less superficially to whatever attracts his attention, you will need to discover types of experience that will arouse his vital interest and challenge him to try to find out exactly what is going on, and then encourage him to talk with you about it. For example, if he is the kind of child who is eager to find out how things work, to take them apart and try to put them together again, but has been too often told, "Don't touch," give him an old alarm clock to pull apart, even though it may never be all put together again. It will give him a new adventure which will lead to interesting conversations. Or, for a younger child, a collection of nuts and bolts or some simple toys that come apart and can be reassembled without too much difficulty will serve to stimulate his thought and very likely arouse questions and encourage conversation that will be in no way superficial.

A child who is less attracted by such mechanical operations may show a special interest in a bug or a beetle that he has found. Instead of just telling him to drop it, you could examine it with him and talk about it and then read or tell him the story of the ant and the grasshopper, or recall the nursery rhyme about the ladybug. Later, when you can find time, you could take him to learn more about bugs at the natural history museum. As a parent enters into whatever enthusiasm his child expresses, supports it with inquiries, suggestions, and explanations and perhaps by providing new related experiences, the level of communication between them will rise above that of the chatterbox and the bored adult.

Such shared activities and talk about them will be of comparable benefit to the child who is less verbal than usual for his age. To express ideas, one needs a talking vocabulary adequate for the situation and the ability to put words into sentences that will convey the intended meaning. Whatever the child's level of verbal expression, parents can help him reach for higher ones. Find time to listen to your child; try to understand not only what he says but what he cannot quite put into words; answer his questions; appreciate his ideas and share some of your own with him. Such communication need not always be on a serious note. In fact, gay and sometimes joking and playful talk back and forth may be more stimulating and give rise to new attempts on your child's part to express himself adequately. As previously noted, vocabulary comes from experience. Development of powers of expression result from the desire to be heard and understood and from practice. Always keep in mind that the development of meaningful verbal expression is essential for learning to read. With proper example and guidance at home, your child will have at least a fair command of language by the time he is six.

Development of personal and social maturity is another factor of importance in preparation for school adjustment and learning to read. While growth along these lines can be fostered by parental guidance, it will also be conditioned somewhat by the child's innate characteristics. Some children are naturally quiet and inclined to daydream, while others are more extroverted. The shy, timid, self-absorbed child needs loving acceptance and gentle encouragement to become more social. The aggressive child needs understanding guidance in controlling and properly directing his drives. Even though individual differences may be great, most children are able to mature at an average rate if the home situation is satisfactory. But even under the best of circumstances, a few children mature at a slower rate. Even their physical growth may not be as rapid as that of the average child. But let us first consider the child's personal and social maturity in terms of his readiness for school at the age of six.

You are hoping that by the time your child will be eager to venture forth to the new experience of entering the first grade and that he will not mind too much being on his own in a strange place among children and adults most of whom he does not know. You hope he will understand and follow directions reasonably well, will not become inattentive or unduly restive before the school day is over and will respond without fear or more than average shyness to his teacher. And, of course, you hope he will not only hold his own with the other children but start to make friends among them. Also, you trust that his teacher will find him prepared for beginning reading so that she need not place him in the group needing further training in reading readiness. What, then, can you as a parent do to realize these hopes for your child's normal maturing during the preschool years?

The following is a summary of the more obvious conditions and provisions which will foster your child's normal growth and development, most of which have been presented in some detail in earlier chapters in somewhat different connections:

1. Provide your child with a comfortable and stimulating home situation. The notion that intelligence or maturity will "out" irrespective of environment is not to he relied upon, even though an occasional "genius" appears to have come from a deprived background.

2. Guard against exposing your child to situations that will seriously frustrate him, for these may cause him to withdraw into himself and avoid activities that will permit normal maturing.

3. Free and stimulating communication between parent and child and between the child and other children and adults will greatly aid his maturing.

4. Sensory as well as intellectual experiences are important, that is, seeing, hearing, smelling, tasting, and touching, in a variety of situations. Widen your child's horizons by acquainting him with what will interest him outside the home in places such as stores, a post office, fire station, airport, and the countryside.

5. Provide opportunities for social interaction between your child and other children and between parents and child in a variety of activities as a means of aiding normal growth.

6. Encouraging and guiding his language development will help your child to mature.

7. Always keep in mind that the happy and relaxed child who knows he is loved and appreciated stands the best chance of developing normally and that his parents are likely to be the best teachers he will ever have.

8. Encourage your child to become self-confident, to act independently when this is appropriate, and to assume his share of responsibility.

9. Maintaining his good health is basic for the proper maturing of your child. This requires a balanced diet, good eating habits, the right amount of sleep and exercise, and above all a comfortable sense of well-being. Any physical disabilities or health problems should receive prompt and adequate attention. Do not expect your child to be of "average" height or weight. Inheritance plays a large part in the relative size of any child and few are exactly average in this or in any other respects.

Parents, therefore, should strive to so shape their child's environment as to encourage natural growth and development toward maturity. Under such favorable conditions as can be provided by most parents, the level of maturity the child will reach by the time he enters first grade is usually sufficient to insure success in his overall school adjustment and in learning to read.

Chapter 10.
Book Experience

Picture books and storybooks with pictures are of interest to preschool children. First attention to picture books begins at about eighteen months of age to two years and increases from then on. Experience with picture books provides good preparation for reading. Pictures for the young child should depict subjects familiar to him, such as, cats, dogs, horses, cars, toys, babies, boys and girls, and adults. They should be drawn simply and clearly. Little children love to look at picture books with their mothers, especially when sitting in her lap and when there is talk by both the mother and child about what they see.

The child of eighteen months will point to an object in the picture and perhaps pat the kitty or try to pick up the ball. Mother can give the name of the object so that her child can say it after her. By two years, the child will be naming some of the items he sees in the picture without any help, such as, a baby, car, or familiar animal. Soon he will begin to talk about them, saying, "See the ball" or "See the dog." The mother can encourage this talk by asking a few simple questions, such as, "Where is the ball?" It is important to get your child to verbalize about what he sees. By the time your child reaches the latter part of the two-year period, he may be able to name all or nearly all the objects depicted and may be making a variety of comments about them, such as, "Baby is sleeping" or "Kitty is pretty."

At an early age, your child can learn to turn pages in the book if you will show him how and encourage him to practice. Also, he will assume that the picture book belongs to him and will carry it around with him as he travels about the house and will go to get it when you offer to look at pictures with him. When he gets a little older, he will sit on the floor and attentively examine some of the pictures by himself, turning one page after another. Near the end of the two-year-period, if encouraged to do so, your child will put his picture book in its proper place on a low shelf. He will be learning to take pride in knowing that the book belongs to him and can be taught to take good care of it. It will not be too soon for him to have more than one book, and he will quickly learn to tell his books apart and to know in which book he will find certain pictures.

At around three years of age, your child is becoming more expert in viewing pictures in his books and his interest in them increases correspondingly. He will note more details, ask more questions, and be more selective as to which picture book or which pictures interest him most at any given time. The parents will soon discover that their child loves repetition, day after day, rather than only going on to new pictures. As he looks again at pictures he has viewed many times before, he may want the parent to repeat any little phrases or rhymes he has come to associate with one picture or another, such as, "Bye, baby, bye" or "The man ran and ran" or "Funny bunny rabbit," or he may repeat them himself. Also, in addition to naming all or nearly all the objects in a picture, he will probably be making a variety of comments about them including observations about what action is taking place, such as, "The girl is putting her doll to bed" or "The bird is flying to the nest." (See "reading" pictures, below.)

Telling or reading stories to your child can go hand in hand with the viewing of pictures. Even the two-year-old enjoys listening to storytelling if the story is kept within the limits of his short attention span. Nursery rhymes are favorites with the very young child, and he loves to have them repeated again and again. Before he can say them himself, he will probably note and correct any errors or changes you may make in the telling. Stories or rhymes will be easier for him to follow and comprehend when they are accompanied by pictures that he can be examining while listening. The pictures may also lead him to make observations of his own and to ask questions. Talking together about the story or rhyme and the pictures will stimulate his thinking and provide valuable practice in verbalizing and communicating. The parent should watch his child carefully during the reading or telling of stories so as to continue only as long as his attention is readily held.

Selection of picture books and stories for the young child is not very difficult. Nursery rhymes continue to be favorites. After some repetitions on different days, your child may join you in at least part of the rhyme. For example, after you say, "Jack and Jill," he may say with you, "went up the hill." By this procedure, many children memorize all their favorite rhymes. Stories such as *Peter Rabbit, The Three Bears,* and *The Hare and the Tortoise* never lose their popularity. There are many modern story and poetry collections, such as the "Little Owl" books and *Poems Children Enjoy* by Elizabeth F. Noon. See Appendix A for a list of books for parents and children to read together. In choosing a book for a young child, keep in mind that the illustrations should be not only colorful and attractive but also simply and clearly drawn. As your child develops, you will also be learning from him what kinds of stories and poems he likes best and his interest and degree of skill in viewing what a picture is all about. When he is four and one-half or five years old, he can help select picture books at the library and will enjoy the story hour which many libraries provide for children of about that age.

When a child has learned to name the objects in a

picture and to make some comments about them including a few observations about what action is taking place, he is ready to begin to "read" the picture more thoroughly. From about three to five years of age, he can acquire considerable skill in describing what is going on in the picture, such as the activity of the characters, the relationships between them, and the role played by the environment. Take for instance the picture of a policeman guiding children across a street. Observations in "reading" this picture may well include: "A policeman is a kind person who helps people. He is showing children how to cross the street safely. The children like the policeman and are pleased to have him look out for them when they cross to the other side of the street. You know he is a policeman because of his blue uniform and his police badge. He looks very tall and strong. The children smile at him and thank him for helping them." Children need some guidance and encouragement while learning to "read" pictures in this manner. When the picture is an illustration of a story, interpreting it will help the child to understand the story when it is read to him. One of the reasons for the many pictures in children's books is to furnish the child with clues as to what is happening in the story that goes with the pictures.

Take another picture of a dog barking at the base of a tree, a cat up in the tree, and a boy running toward the dog. To read the picture, the child must recognize that the dog has treed the cat, and the boy is coming to the rescue. The child may appreciate that the cat is afraid to come down, that dogs like to chase cats, but that the boy does not want his dog to frighten the cat and will probably get the dog to go away from the tree so that the cat can come down safely.

Training in interpretation of pictures should begin with relatively simple action pictures. By gradual progression, your child will learn to interpret more and more complex pictures provided they present situations with which he has had some personal experience. If he has been on picnics and has either camped in the woods or has seen others camping, he will be able, between five and six years of age, to describe a camping picture more or less as follows: "The family has gone on a camping trip in a park. Dad, with the help of the boys, is setting up the tent. Their dog is chasing a rabbit through the bushes. Mother and the little girl are putting food on a spread-out cloth, getting ready for lunch. Some fishing poles are leaning up against the car, and there is a brook nearby, so after lunch they are probably going fishing."

Experience in interpreting or "reading" pictures is very valuable in preparing your child for reading. All good textbooks used in beginning reading have many pictures closely related to the text. Examination of these pictures gives many context clues to what is said in print. Unless your child has learned to see the details in a picture, to note any action taking place, and to think about and try to interpret the relationships between the characters by the time he enters the first grade, he will be handicapped in learning to read.

By the time your child is five years old, he should have several books of his very own, both picture books and storybooks. He will need a shelf or other appropriate place to keep them, and he should be encouraged to keep them there when they are not in use. You should train him to take good care of his books, not tearing the pages or getting them dirty. Much of his attitude toward his books will reflect that of his parents toward their books. Whenever you acquire a new book, show it to him and let him admire it with you. Perhaps you can tell him something about it and why you are glad to have it. If you use a bookmark instead of turning down the page to mark your place, he, too, will want to do this with his books. This training in the care of his books will make it easy for him later on to conform to school regulations about keeping his textbooks in good condition for those who will use them after he is through with them. It will also foster pride in the possession of attractive, well-kept books as a start toward a library of his very own.

As your child approaches school age, he will have developed a rather wide range of interests about which you can find material to read to him. You will be guided by these interests in selecting books to enjoy together and will also introduce new subjects from time to time whenever it seems appropriate and you can locate suitable material. Books about animals are almost always popular. One of these is *Animals Every Child Should Know,* by Dena Humphreys. Preschool children like stories about transportation, such as *The Little Fire Engine* by Lois Lenski, and the numerous ones about trains, trucks and cars, airplanes, boats, and horses. Material about outdoor life holds the interest of many childen, provided they have had some direct experience with vegetation in parks and the countryside, bodies of water, such as brooks and rivers, lakes and perhaps the ocean, different types of landscape such as mountains and valleys and perhaps the desert and sandy beaches, and with what farming is all about. Two books in this group are *Come to the Country* by Grace Paul and *The Brave Cowboy* by Joan Walsh Anglund. For the country child who has made a trip to a city, Lois Lenski's *We Live in the City* might hold special interest. Scientific subjects have great appeal to some children, such as books about the seasons, how plants grow from seed, care of pets, the life of wild animals and birds, magnetism (provide a magnet and paper clips, tacks, etc.), and what can be seen under a microscope. Books for preschool children relating to some of these subjects are: *The Doubleday First Guide to Birds,* by Sabra Kimball and Heathcote Kimball; *Brian Wildsmith's Wild Animals* by Brian Wildsmith; *Secret Places* by D. J. Arneson; and *Weather* by Leslie Waller. (See Appendix A for complete list of recommended books.)

While, as mentioned above, your child needs to have had some prior experience with the subjects about which you read to him, it is also a good idea to supplement the stories read by additional related experiences. Thus, after reading about plants and how they grow, arrange for him to plant some seeds so that he can see for himself how they sprout and push up through the soil and then develop leaves and perhaps flowers. For city dwellers, parks and nurseries offer opportunities to observe a wide variety of plants in various stages of growth. Stories about wild animals and birds will become more meaningful after a trip to the zoo or the natural history museum, even though your child has visited both these places before. A visit to a pet shop or a farm and, if possible, a look through a microscope are other ways to add depth of meaning to subjects related to these activities. And throughout the whole process of enjoying the stories read to him about subjects he's especially interested in as well as the trips you take to learn more about these subjects, your child will have questions to ask and comments to make. You should do your best to answer his questions and should encourage spontaneous conversation between the two of you about the stories and whatever is seen or done in connection with them.

A picture dictionary, such as *My First Golden Dictionary* (Golden Press), is a worthwhile addition to any young child's library. It provides a wealth of interesting pictures which provide good subjects for conversation. For example, on the last page you will find pictures of a xylophone, yarn, a zebra, a zipper, and animals in the zoo. Perhaps your child has a *xylophone*, a fairly common toy for very young children. *Yarn* may be a new word but you can show him that his sweater and his socks are knitted with it. The *zebra* looks like a striped horse. He surely knows about *zippers* and has probably been to the *zoo*. Perhaps he is ready to be interested in the letters *x*, *y*, and *z* which appear separately at the sides of the pictures, and you can read the words and the definitions to him. Use only two or three pages at a time and encourage questions and talk about each picture. The picture dictionary will be useful in the activities described in Chapters 11 and 12. After you and your child have gone all through the book, present it to him to keep with his other books. He will enjoy thumbing through it frequently.

In reading to your child it is a good plan to select material variously from nursery rhymes, stories, nature-study subjects, scientific accounts, and descriptions of family outings and other activities. In this way you will be helping to widen his range of interests and to develop his reading tastes. While the selection of material unfamiliar to him must be yours, he, too, should be allowed to make some selections. The more conversation that develops around whatever is read, the more value it is likely to have for your child. He will gain in understanding and in verbal facility and will learn to listen more thoughtfully.

Your child's contact with books, looking at the pictures, and listening to the stories read to him will probably stimulate him to tell his own stories. For example, the picture of a butterfly and a story about its coming out of a cocoon may recall to him a story he's heard about chasing butterflies with a net or the butterfly exhibit at the natural history museum where pushing a button turns on a light that makes the butterfly wings shine like oil on water with many colors. This may lead him to thinking and talking about how he might make himself a butterfly net with a rod of some sort, some wire, and some cloth and string. The imaginative child may develop a butterfly story of his own. Enjoy his story whether it is factual or imaginative and try to add one of your own. Such an exchange of ideas and their elaboration stimulates creative thought, develops ease in verbal expression, and provides practice in communicating with others.

In learning to read, it is necessary to develop the habit of moving the eyes from left to right along a line of print. During the preschool period, a beginning can be made in teaching this left-to-right movement. Picture stories for children are made with the first picture at the left, the next one to the right, and so on to the end of the line. When you first show your child picture stories, point to the first one, then after viewing and discussing it, point to the next picture to the right, and so on. Soon, he can point with you, and before long, after a moderate amount of guidance, he will catch on so that further pointing is not necessary. Comics that are published for young children provide good practice in this left-to-right progression. Forming this habit before entering the first grade will make it much easier for your child to follow the lines of print on the page when he is beginning to learn to read. He also needs to learn which is his right hand and which is his left one. (See Chapter 8 for a discussion of this subject.)

Book experience, as outlined in this chapter, first of all develops an interest in books and acquaints your child with some of the enjoyment they can provide. He will learn how to interpret pictures and will develop the habits of attention necessary for following a story as you read it to him. Also, he will discover that print "talks." Consequently, he will be eager to learn how to read that print himself when he enters grade one or perhaps kindergarten. (See Chapter 12.) The child is fortunate whose parents take the trouble during the preschool years to give him a generous amount of book experience, who see that he has a few books of his very own, teach him to care for them properly and to treasure and enjoy them. This will prepare him in many ways for beginning reading when he enters school.

Book experience does not include teaching your child to read words. The parents are not, therefore, involved in any formal teaching of reading. Very few parents have the training to do this well, and most children are not ready for beginning reading during the preschool years. Some are not even ready when they enter school. A few children on their own will make a start at reading before going to school. It is all right for them to do so, but it is unwise to push them in any way. The parent's role is to acquaint their child with the pleasure to be derived from books and to help him develop skill in interpreting pictures and habits of listening and talking about the stories read to him.

Chapter 11.
The Five- and Six-Year-Old

The five-year-old will probably go to kindergarten, and the six-year-old will begin grade one. When their child begins school, the parents should keep in close contact with his teacher and the school situation. In a well-organized modern kindergarten, your child will develop rather rapidly in many ways. His eye-hand and other muscular coordinations will improve, and he will acquire more advanced language skills. Also, he will gain in his ability to follow directions, to complete a task, to work independently, and to cooperate with other children. He may even begin to learn to read. (This is discussed in Chapter 12.)

Several authorities have emphasized that we are ready for a careful study of the traditional kindergarten. Dolores Durkin in *Children Who Read Early* (Teachers College Press) found that wide diversity exists in opinions and practices in present-day kindergartens. Many kindergartens are the same as they were thirty years ago when use of paper and pencils was forbidden because it was thought that five-year-olds were not "ready" for them. At the other extreme, some kindergartens are poor imitations of first grade. Neither seems appropriate. There is already much evidence that school administrators should move away from traditional kindergarten programs toward modern methods based on research and experience as to what is appropriate for the instruction of five-year-olds of the present generation. Whatever the general plan, the kindergarten teacher must first determine what the child has learned at home and then proceed from there to prepare him for formal reading instruction. The child in kindergarten should not be in an environment devoid of verbal symbols. It seems reasonable that he should be exposed to some written words. Much growth towards reading can be effected through casual contacts during the school day with printed verbal material, such as the names of the children in the room, labels on boxes of supplies, and a word or two under a picture on the bulletin board. While many children arrive in kindergarten not ready to begin reading, some are ready, and a few may even be reading simple material. The task of the teacher is to provide challenge and help for every child in her class. (See Chapter 12.) The discussion in this chapter supports the view that the present-day kindergarten should represent an advance from the traditional program.

Some of the activities in the kindergarten are extensions of what your child has been learning at home. He will receive further training in lengthening his attention span, in eye-hand coordination, and in auditory and visual perception. His abilities in language and comprehension will be developed. He will be encouraged to ask questions and to take an active part in discussions. There will be field trips, games, songs, and storytelling. Frequently, the teacher will read aloud to the class. The child whose parents have already provided him with many enjoyable experiences along these lines will enter readily into these kindergarten activities. Adjusting to being one of a group of children of his own age and to a teacher other than his mother may be a somewhat new experience for him. Much will depend upon how well he has learned to respect the rights of others, to cooperate and share with his playmates, and to feel at ease with understanding adults other than those in his own family.

You will want to keep in close touch with what your child is experiencing in kindergarten. He will come home with much to tell you about what has happened during the day and sometimes with new ideas, questions, and perhaps concern about some incident that disturbed or annoyed him. He may also proudly bring to show you something he made or a picture he drew. Whenever possible, be ready to listen, advise, and admire right away. If your child gets the idea that you are not very much interested, he will tend to give up the practice of telling you in detail whatever happened at school that seemed of importance to him. That would be unfortunate for you both.

To help your child succeed in school, you will also need to acquaint yourself with his particular school and with its place in the educational plan of the community. The kindergarten teacher needs and wants your help and will welcome a visit from you about four weeks after school starts. You need not wait for an invitation but should allow time for the teacher to get to know your child and to observe how he is adjusting to school. If, during these early weeks, your child is showing any unusual difficulty in adapting to the kindergarten program, the teacher will get in touch with you. Similarly, should you become aware that your child is not getting off to a good start at school, you need not delay in making contact with his teacher. Especially during the first few years of school, teacher and parent should work closely together. And when your child knows that you make visits to his school and consult with his teacher, he will feel that home and school are closely related and that you are sharing with him appropriate parts of his school life. (See also Chapter 13.)

When parent and teacher meet, they can exchange information and impressions about the child and together consider any changes or additions to his activities or adjustments in their ways of working with him that may seem desirable. You can report on your child's attitudes toward school as expressed at home; health problems, if any; his interests and abilities as you have observed them in relation to books, TV programs, play, tasks assigned to him, and the like; how he gets along with other members of the family and with playmates; and any fears or other emotional problems he may be having in relation to school or to situations at home. The teacher can tell you how well your child is learning, what part he takes in group activities and discussions, and how he gets along with his classmates and with her. She will have noted to what extent he is able to listen attentively, understand directions, observe rules, and work independently. And in these and other respects, she will indicate in what ways he is improving and in what areas he may need further assistance at school and at home. You can ask the teacher about books, TV programs, phonograph records, and community resources which may be helpful to your child and to you in working with him. And do not hesitate to call on the principal when you feel the need for his help and advice.

The major part of a modern kindergarten program is designed to prepare the child for reading and the main objective in grade one is teaching the child to read. Parents are partners in any reading program. When their child enters kindergarten, they have already spent about five years preparing him for school. And after he starts school, he will continue to spend more time at home than in school which will take up only about a third of each day for five days a week during not over forty weeks a year. It is therefore clear that much of every child's educational experience will continue to be centered in the home.

Parents serve as examples for their child. He loves them, looks up to them, and usually wants to do as they do. If they have good speech habits, he will learn to speak correctly. His interest in books will tend to reflect theirs. Children of five and six love to work along with their mothers in the kitchen or with their fathers in the yard or garage or around the house. Many of the usual activities in the home can give your child not only pleasure but also learning experiences that will directly or indirectly interest him in reading and contribute to his reading skills.

A child of five can usually select his favorite cereal package and will soon recognize not only the pictures but also the name on the box. He can learn to fill a measuring cup full, or even half full, and will enjoy finding out for himself how many cups of water it takes to fill a quart measure. You can teach him to distinguish a teaspoon from a tablespoon and how to fill either level full. With some types of can openers, he can open a can. Let him select a can of soup, open it, and with or without your help empty it into a saucepan and add a cup of water or milk. Together, you can then heat it for him. Soon he will recognize the printed name on the can of some of the soups he likes and will be trying to read the directions for preparing it.

Not long after your child has really started to read, you can help him follow simple recipes, such as those on the package of a pancake mix which you may even simplify as follows: 1 c. mix, 1 c. milk, 1 egg, 1 t. oil, put in shaker and shake 10 times. Or you may select recipes of your own, such as a standard one for popovers which will probably read about as follows: Beat together just until smooth: 1 c. sifted flour, ½ t. salt, 1 c. milk, 2 eggs. Fill well greased deep muffin pans ¾ full. Bake at 425°. After helping him a few times in preparing the batter, let him set the oven at the right temperature, do the measuring and mixing by himself, and then join with him in watching over the baking. Boys are apt to be as interested in cooking as girls, and both will like to accumulate their own recipes in individual recipe boxes. They can copy them from your recipes.

A child of five or six is also fascinated by kitchen appliances some of which have printed guides on them. After watching each appliance work and with a little help from you, he will soon distinguish between such words as *off, cold, warm, hot, wash* and *rinse* on the washing machine, *gas* and *broil* on your oven, and perhaps *blend, mix,* and *whip* on your electric mixer. And if you have a set of labeled containers, he may add *bread, sugar, coffee,* and *tea* to his sight vocabulary.

Similarly, a son or a daughter of five or six delights in working with his father. Long before a young child can work independently at such tasks as washing the car, setting out plants, or putting up a new shelf in house or garage, he can become a good helper, carrying some of the tools, picking up whatever is accidently dropped, holding a small board in place for a minute or two, polishing parts of the car that he can easily reach, or breaking up some of the lumps in the soil being prepared for new plants. He will be getting valuable practice in following directions and in developing good work habits, as well as having a fine time with his father. On a drive in the car to the hardware store, he can look for words he knows on the dashboard, such as *lights, brake, washer,* and he can watch for traffic signs to see if he can read some or all of them. At the store, he may very well help his father find the item he is looking for and may take note of its printed name. When their work for the day is done, the father can talk it over with his son or daughter, pointing out that the reason he keeps his tools in order is so that he can find them next time. They can talk about how he plans his work and the satisfaction of getting everything cleaned up afterward.

The child in kindergarten or first grade can participate more fully than at an earlier age in the celebration of holidays, birthdays, and other special days with cookie-making, gift-wrapping, Christmas-tree trimming, planning a costume for Halloween and making a jack-o'-lantern. Writing or printing on a gift whom it is for and who gives it may now have become possible with a little help. Making place cards for a party will be fun for a first-grader if he is given a printed list of the names to copy from. And it won't be long before your child can read the names of family members well enough to have the honor of distributing some of the gifts from the Christmas tree or at Chanukah time.

During this same period your child's interest in books, selected television shows, and planned trips to places he may or may not have visited before will grow and expand. While still enjoying familiar stories, songs, and places to visit, he will be ready and eager for more advanced experiences along these lines. Good possibilities for widening his horizons include trips to a fair, an athletic event, a horse show or rodeo, an island or other location reached by a boat, or attending a children's concert. And, as in the preschool years, outlining in advance what he is to look for and talking the trip over afterward will enhance its value to him.

In working and talking with the children in her class, the kindergarten teacher is likely to discover early which ones have parents who have been actively preparing their child for school. Unless the child is still fearful of expressing himself in the presence of so many others and to a teacher who has not yet won his confidence, he will be telling about the live lion he saw like the one in the picture or showing that he already knows how to measure with a yardstick or be asking questions which reflect attentiveness, some prior knowledge, and good habits of thinking about what he sees or hears. She will probably find that her kindergartners range from children like this one to a few at the other extreme who are obviously immature, dependent, and rather helpless. They may cry easily, not speak above a whisper, and may seem unfamiliar with books and unable to perceive details in pictures or to understand and follow any but the most simple directions. The majority of her children will be performing in the middle range between these two extremes.

While the kindergarten teacher is well aware that there are individual differences in the rates at which children develop even under the best of circumstances, she will do well to determine as soon as possible which children need more help at home. Many parents are both capable and willing to give such assistance but cannot do so without guidance and encouragement. Some can do much more for their child than they have been doing, once they understand what is needed and how they can go about providing it. All but perhaps a very few can and will follow some of the suggestions of their child's teacher. After the teacher has met and talked with at least one of the child's parents, she can judge what initial suggestions will be most appropriate. A continuing teacher-parent relationship can then be fostered by occasional conferences, notes back and forth, and now and then a telephone conversation. Some school systems provide for group conferences with parents of children in kindergarten and first grade to acquaint them with the various steps in the program planned for their children at school and to talk over common problems.

Kindergarten programs vary from place to place, as mentioned earlier. Paul McKee and M. Lucile Harrison have published a program for teachers to use with pupils on *Getting Ready to Read* (Houghton Mifflin Company). Some of their material will be used as a basis for the following discussion.

One kind of early training in the kindergarten serves to improve listening and increase verbal facility. Spoken context may be used to do this. For instance, the teacher may say, "At dinner we sit on a _____." The child is asked to complete the sentence so that it sounds right.

He may say "chair" or perhaps "stool." The teacher accepts any word that makes sense. The parent, as a game, may make up sentences in a similar manner. Usually, there are several words to choose from in completing the sentence so that it makes sense. Accept any good one. And let your child try to make up sentences for you to give the last word. It must be kept in mind that while some children will catch on quickly to this use of verbal context, others will need further explanation and practice. Exercises in spoken context can be fun games.

Throughout the kindergarten period your child will receive practice in the left-to-right progress in looking at pictures and in other exercises. This left-to-right viewing will become absolutely essential in reading lines of print. Here, too, parents can supplement the school program by selected home activities with their child. As mentioned before, certain comics in newspapers provide good practice in left-to-right viewing. The parent can read the messages in the balloons as the child follows the story in the successive pictures from left to right. Comic strips that may interest your child are: *The Ryatts, Peanuts, Nancy,* and perhaps *Beatle Bailey.* Certain comic books are also useful.

When a child in kindergarten does not seem able to follow directions, the teacher searches for the reason or reasons. Does he understand what she says? He may have a slight hearing difficulty, or perhaps cannot see clearly the markings on the chalkboard she is using to illustrate her directions. Or he may not be familiar with some of the words she is using. Another language may be more commonly used at home or for other reasons, he may have acquired only a limited vocabulary. Or he may have difficulty in paying attention. Whatever his problem, once the teacher discovers its nature, she will try to help him with it and, when indicated, will call it to the attention of his parents and enlist their assistance.

Your child will also be taught number symbols as a part of the kindergarten program. This needs to be done only with those pupils who do not yet recognize the numbers 1 to 10. The preferred procedure is to start off with about the numbers *1*, *2*, and *3*. They can be on cards or on the chalkboard. The numbers should be in sequence from left to right. The pupils point to a digit and name it with whatever help is necessary. Then give each child three cards with one of these numbers printed on each and have them arrange the cards in proper sequence. Another exercise will be to find pages *1*, *2*, and *3* in a book, telling them to look at the top or the bottom of the page to find the number. At later sessions, work with the digits *4*, *5*, and *6*, and so on until all numbers through *10* are learned in their written form. When the pupils have learned the number symbols in sequence, they can practice finding individual numbers and can learn to write them, first by copying and then from memory.

Teaching letters of the alphabet is now rather common in many kindergartens. McKee and Harrison, cited above, have outlined a good method for doing this. Use a group of capital letters such as *D*, *F*, *G*, *I*, *M*, *U*. They need not be in alphabetic order, for most five-year-olds are not yet ready to learn the letters in sequence. Print each letter on duplicate cards, one letter to a card. Give each of six pupils in a group one card, keeping the duplicates for your own use. Place one of your letters on its card in the pocket of a pocket chart, saying "This is __ (naming the letter). If you have __, come and place it in the pocket below mine." Then, ask the child to name the letter. Continue with the other letters.

The next step will be for you to name the letter without showing your card. Pass out the cards as before and say, "I want the letter __." Ask the child who has it to come and place the letter in the top pocket of the chart. Do the same with another letter and then ask who can name the two letters now placed. Continue with other letters. Repeat the whole series. Then, put all six letters in the chart and ask the children to name them in order, as you point at them from left to right. Change the order of the letters in the chart and repeat. In talking about the letters, the teacher says, "This is capital *B*," etc. Continue the exercise on successive days until all the six capital letters are learned. Carry out the same kind of exercise with the lower-case letters that correspond to the capital letters used above. Use the term "small letters" in referring to them. Suggest that the pupils start at the left and move to the right in naming the letters. In later lessons for recognizing letter forms, use the same six used above but mix capital with lower-case letters. Call attention to the difference in shape between the small letters and their corresponding capital letters.

Another exercise that has a place in the kindergarten is teaching the pupils to "listen" to the beginning sounds in words. Select a group of four or five words that begin the same, such as *mother, milk, monkey, man, meat, mat, moon.* It will be helpful to have pictures of what is represented by the words. Some children readily grasp the idea of words that begin alike, that is, with the same sound. Others will recognize the similarity only after repeated practice. A variation of this exercise is to start with a word such as *man* and then change the first letter to give a different sound and make a different word, such as *man, can, fan, pan.* Call attention to each different sound and to the different word it makes. Here, too, showing pictures of the subjects named is a good idea. This is a difficult exercise for some children. For those who continue to make mistakes, individual help will be necessary.

Another way to teach letter-sound association is to use a form of spoken context. Speak a sentence with the last word left out. Hold up a letter the pupils know and ask for a word to complete the sentence that makes sense and begins with the sound of the letter you are showing. For example, say, "I see an animal with four legs and he is a ____," and hold up the letter *d*. Exercises of this kind can be supplemented by telling the children a little story, the last word of which they are to guess from the letter you hold up. For example: "Jim went to the circus and saw clowns, lions, and many other animals. When he came home and had his supper, he was so tired he could hardly keep his eyes open so he gladly went to ____." (Holding up the letter *b*.) Or, you can write the last word on the chalkboard and call attention to the first letter. From the context, most but not all of the children will "guess" what the proper word is.

It will now be time to teach more letter forms and sounds. Use about six letters and the same types of exercises used with letters taught earlier. Then, as before, teach beginning sounds of words that start with one of the new letters. If possible, show pictures with names that begin with the various new letters. As new letters are taught and practiced in exercises, intersperse them with letters learned earlier. After the single letters are mastered, progress to the consonant blends, such as *th, sh, ch, wh*. Work with about four consonant blends at a time, using methods along the same lines as those employed with single letters. Mastering consonant blends will be more difficult than learning the single letters and, therefore, will require more practice and more opportunities for frequent review. The McKee and Harrison reference cited above provides a detailed guide for a prereading kindergarten program, only parts of which are presented here in abbreviated form. Other parts of their report will be referred to in Chapter 12. Another good reference for kindergarten teachers and for the teaching of beginners in first grade is *Foundations for Reading*, by Marion Monroe and Bernice Rogers. (Scott, Foresman and Company.)

Opinions differ somewhat as to the advisability of acquainting parents with methods of prereading instruction such as illustrated above and with how reading is taught in the early grades. Some fear that to do so will encourage parents to consider themselves expert reading teachers. But more and more educators are finding that when parents become partners with the school in its reading program they quickly learn to distinguish between their role and that of the teacher. And teachers in a school reading program that values and provides for parent understanding and assistance find that the child whose parents know how to help him practice his newly acquired prereading or reading skills at home gains thereby.

To acquire as many informed and interested parents as possible to support and supplement the school reading program, school administrators and teachers need to consult with representative parents in the district as to what methods might be most promising. Individual parent-teacher conferences are not enough. And prepared talks to groups of parents are seldom as well attended or as productive as properly led group discussions with some audiovisual illustrations of some of the methods a teacher uses in prereading and reading instruction and of how skills acquired in this manner can be practiced at home in games and various activities other than drills regarded as "homework." In some school systems some parents actually help in the classroom for brief or longer periods as a sort of in-service training. They may make recordings, print words on cards, mount pictures, or actually work with individual children as directed by the teacher. Parents also often assist in field trips but too often are called upon only to help with the transportation and act as general overseer of the group as it moves from place to place. Whenever possible, the parent or parents should attend the teacher-pupil planning session for the trip so that they can intelligently help in fulfilling the purposes of the trip. They should also be welcome to participate in the class discussion of the trip afterward. It is a special event in any family when a child first starts kindergarten. The school will do well to seek to enlist and activate full parent-school cooperation at this time by means of a planned program to be modified as the occasion arises.

The initial levels or reading instruction in grade one will depend upon how much the pupils have learned in the kindergarten prereading program. Even if all the children had attended the same kindergarten, individual differences in their degrees of preparedness for reading would soon become apparent to their first-grade teacher. She will need to do some grouping to provide properly for the pupils not yet ready for reading, others who are ready, and the few who can already read. These groupings will be somewhat fluid, so that at least two of the three may do certain exercises together and a child in any group may be moved temporarily, or for a more extended period, to another group whenever his teacher judges such a move to be to the child's advantage. And all groups should work together on class projects and share in other nonreading activities.

The reading-readiness program started in the kindergarten will be continued at ever advancing levels even after the children start reading and from then on, as all pupils will need some preparation for reading each new unit and for beginning a new subject. The exact procedures used in the reading instruction itself in grade one will vary somewhat from school to school and teacher to teacher but will ordinarily include: the development of a sight vocabulary by use of experience charts which may relate to a class project, such as constructing an Indian camp or a farmyard; words on cards, a bulletin board or chalkboard; word games and other devices; use of preprimers and primers, very possibly from a basic reading series; use of supplementary reading material, such as script texts; chart work for developing visual discrimination and word perception; primers and easy books other than the basic text; and the carrying forward of word-recognition techniques begun in kindergarten by exercises in noting beginning and ending sounds of words and "guessing" a word from the context.

By the time the average child has reached the end of grade one, he will have acquired quite a stock of sight words, some ability in word-recognition techniques, and considerable skill in both oral and silent reading of easy materials. His achievement, at whatever level, will reflect not only his natural ability but also the extent to which both parents and teachers have helped him to develop it.

Let us now reconsider and summarize what parents can contribute to the development of their child during the five- and six-year-period. By this time your child will have acquired a number of interests and enthusiasms of his own and will be able to talk with you about them and to express his ideas much more freely than at earlier ages. In general, your role as his parent is an extension of what has gone before, but it now becomes of increasing importance to keep alert to what interests him most and to be prepared for fairly frequent changes in interests. Also, as he makes friends at school and in the neighborhood, keeping in touch with his associations and activities outside the home may require special attention and effort on your part. Specifically, the parents of the five- and six-year-old child should try to do the following:

1. Maintain good communication with your child. Show that you are interested in what he does in and out of school. Be willing to listen sympathetically to whatever he tells you about his experiences, his troubles, and his contacts with others.

2. Encourage conversation with your child. Share with him what has happened in your day that he might like to hear, talk over plans for the weekend, or tell him a joke. When he shows a new interest, tell him what you know about it and help him find out more about it. Encourage his questions and do your best to answer them satisfactorily.

3. Take your child on trips to familiar places and to places new to him, as well. Now that he is older, he will see and understand more than at an earlier time and will be interested in places and activities that did not particularly appeal to him at three and four. Plan the trips with him in advance, perhaps allowing him to invite a friend or two to go along, answer any questions raised during the trip, and talk it all over with him afterward. Whenever you can, supplement what he has seen and heard by supplying additional information and reading to him about related subjects. You will be helping him to increase his vocabulary, develop new ideas, and expand his knowledge about the world he lives in, thus adding to his reading readiness.

4. Your child is now able to perform a number of tasks about the home and yard. He can be given responsibility for certain specific ones but will probably need to be reminded to do them. They should be comfortably within his ability and such that he understands their importance, even though he may not be particularly interested in some of them. He knows that someone has to set the table, carry out the trash, and make the beds. Besides doing his share of such routine tasks, he should have some work to do which he regards as fun, or at least as a privilege, such as helping to make cookies or to wash the car. And he should feel responsible for hanging up his own clothes and putting his toys away.

5. Even after he begins to read, stories should be read aloud to him. Some of them should be of his own choosing,

while others may introduce him to new material. At this age, he is apt to especially like factual material about Indians, the growth of plant and trees, what is in the ocean, details about transportation on land and water and in the air, and explanations of gravity or how a magnet works. Some children delight in the imagery and rhythms found in poems. Your child will like to have a definite story time to look forward to, as well as surprise times when stories are read to him.

6. Although he may need some help occasionally, your child can now dress and undress himself, learn to tie a bow if he has not already done so, take a shower, comb his hair, and do various other personal tasks. You should expect and encourage him to do these things.

7. Your child can profit by further training in listening. The development of good habits of listening and the increase of his attention span can be fostered by the methods described in Chapter 7. The training consists largely of gauging the length of your conversations with him and your reading sessions by the closeness or wavering of his attention. You will find that when he is deeply interested in the subject he will listen attentively for quite a bit longer than he was able to do at three and four. Although training in the kindergarten and first grade will aim at developing good listening habits, your activities at home can supplement what is done in school.

8. In general, remember that you are still your child's best teacher and do not turn over to the school the whole program of teaching your child to read. Keep in mind that the teacher in kindergarten or first grade has twenty to thirty children of five or six, while you have only one or two.

9. The social training of your child is largely your responsibility, although the school does provide valuable supervised group experience. You are fortunate if there

are other children in the immediate neighborhood of about the age of your child. Otherwise it will be up to you to make special arrangements for him to meet children elsewhere and spend a fair amount of time with them. Attending Sunday School or classes in swimming or nature study or the like may help to meet his social needs.

10. As discussed in more detail in other chapters, you can supplement the instruction your child is receiving in schools in many ways. You can extend his earlier activities in learning to distinguish different shapes and sounds, manipulate toys, use scissors and other appropriate tools, follow directions, work independently or with others, name colors, tell time, "read" pictures, and talk about what he sees, hears, and thinks about. In addition, you can supplement more specifically whatever he is just learning in school, provided you are careful to coordinate your efforts with those of his teacher. For example, when she is teaching him to recognize capital letters and to distinguish them from those in lower case, she will probably welcome having him practice doing this at home under your guidance. Or, when he is learning consonant blends, you can encourage him to find ones he knows in stories you read to him, or on cereal packages or signs when you are driving in the car.

Upon first reading these suggestions as to your role with your child of five or six, you may feel that too much is expected of you. But certainly you are already performing many of these functions as a matter of course, even though sometimes you have not realized the importance of what you have been doing naturally. And probably you can make use of some of these suggestions to round out your own program of teaching your child what you realize he needs to learn to do well in kindergarten and grade one.

Chapter 12.
Reading in the Kindergarten

During recent years there has been a movement toward teaching formal reading in the kindergarten. Many approve such a program and many oppose it. The difficulty in making a clear decision on when children should begin to read is well illustrated by Dolores Durkin in "When Should Children Begin to Read," in the *Sixty Seventh Yearbook of the National Society for the Study of Education* (University of Chicago Press) and *Children Who Read Early* (Teachers College Press). The question of when to begin reading is a very complicated one. It is concerned largely with the marked differences in the development of children of the same chronological age. Five-year-olds show great variation in what they already know and in what they can and want to do.

In some areas, teaching reading in the kindergarten has become very popular. That popularity may interfere with the making of intelligent decisions about the kindergarten program. The tendency to assume that all five-year-olds are ready to learn to read is a dangerous one. And often the reading program in the kindergarten is too much like the standard first-grade program which is too formal for most five-year-olds. On the other hand, the traditional kindergarten program tends to lack any opportunity for learning to read. Very likely it consists only of activities that some, and perhaps many, children of kindergarten age have already outgrown and abandoned. These children tend to be disappointed with what they find in kindergarten and too often their year spent there is a dull one offering little challenge and arousing only occasional interest. If a child has not attended nursery school, the traditional kindergarten program of singing, storytelling, coloring, and games may interest him for a while but very likely not for a whole school year. Modern school programs provide for careful evaluation of the preschool experiences of the children entering kindergarten so that no time need be lost in unnecessary repetition of what they have already learned. Instead, the teacher will undertake with skill and understanding to meet the various needs of her pupils for new experiences and for opportunity to progress toward first-grade work. Children who are found to be ready for beginning reading upon entering kindergarten or later in the year will receive appropriate reading instruction. That is, the instruction will be less formal than that provided in the first grade and carefully adapted to the interests and behavior patterns of the five-year-old. There may be no daily set schedule for reading and play activities with oral language and sounds may be used to develop preliminary reading skills. (See below.) And the few children who are already reading simple material upon entering kindergarten will be given special opportunity to progress at their own rate.

Although the kindergarten teacher undertakes to provide help and challenge for every child in her class, how is she able to accomplish this? First of all, the class must be small enough to permit individualized instruction. And much depends upon factors in the child's environment, that is, his background of experience before entering school. The teacher will also need the continuing interest and cooperation of the parents both in the support of the school program and in providing their child with appropriate growth experiences outside of school hours. Some of the questions as to when and how to begin the teaching of reading which are of concern to both parents and teachers will now be discussed.

At what age should a child be taught to read? According to Glenn Doman in *How to Teach Your Baby to Read* (Random House), even babies can be taught to read.

And for a long time it has been known that children of a mental age of four years can be taught to read. Certainly children of a mental age of five years can learn to read, provided the method of teaching and the selection of materials are suited to their interests and abilities and their preschool experiences have been adequate. There seems to be no specific level of mental maturity above which few fail in reading and below which a relatively large proportion fail, provided the reading program is properly adjusted to the abilities of the pupils.

The possibility of teaching reading to babies excites parents and disturbs educators. And the question arises, why teach two-, three-, and four-year-old children to read? Is it because the child desires it, or the mother? What does it do to the very young child? The answers to these questions are discussed by C. M. McCullough and me in our book, *Teaching Elementary Reading* (Appleton-Century-Crofts). Unless restricted, young children tend to engage in spontaneous activities, play with other children, use their imagination, and learn to think. Sitting still and being taught to read does not come naturally to children from two to four years of age. A heavy emphasis upon reading instruction at these ages tends to isolate the child from many of the experiences he needs to develop normally. And teaching a baby to read has little or nothing to do with the activities he seeks and needs during infancy. It is the mother, not the child, who is motivated to make any such attempt. She may have been misguided by someone whose opinion she regards as expert or may just be overeager to have her baby excel. It is unfortunate when her ambition, rather than the best interests of her child, determines any course of action. There is, however, a difference between forcing a very young child to try to read and helping the occasional child who is a self-starter, that is, whose own inner drive motivates him to insist upon learning to read at an unusually early age. While a child does not profit from forced learning, he does maintain and use skills acquired as a result of his own interest and enthusiasm.

Let us now consider in more detail kindergarten programs as related to reading, with special reference to one extensive study made of several approaches to this problem. What is to be provided in the kindergarten besides beginning reading instruction for those children who are ready for it upon entrance or later on in the year? For the class as a whole, there should be training to prepare them for first-grade reading. Much of this training includes development of verbal facility, concept building, some word-recognition skills, left-to-right word orientation, auditory discrimination, experience with oral sentence patterns, comprehension and interpretation, elementary study skills, and a widening of interests. Early stages of some of these skills will have been learned prior to school, as described in previous chapters. Kindergarten activities supplement and advance them.

Many attempts have been made to teach reading at the kindergarten level. The most thorough of these is reported by Paul McKee, Joseph E. Brzeinski and M. Lucile Harrison in *The Effectiveness of Teaching Reading in Kindergarten* (The Denver Public Schools, 1966, Cooperative Research Project No. 5-0371). A somewhat detailed summary of the report follows.

The primary purpose of the study was to discover the effectiveness of teaching reading during the kindergarten year and the degree to which this affected reading in grades one to five. Also, an attempt was made to discover whether such training was harmful or beneficial.

First, it was noted that several studies have found that the age at which reading can be taught depends upon the methods and materials used. In addition, it seemed that level of maturity (mental age) was not a determining factor for beginning to read, except for children who are mentally retarded. Also, difficulties some children have in auditory and visual discrimination can be overcome by training.

The preliminary part of the program was to teach the kindergarten pupils the skills basic to beginning reading, as described in *Getting Ready to Read*, referred to in Chapter 11. These skills are: (1) Using only spoken context as a clue to the desired word, as, "Johnny drank his _____ (*milk, juice, water, coke*)." The pupils supplied any word that made sense. (2) Listening for beginning consonant sounds. (3) Distinguishing letter forms from one another. (4) Using oral context and the beginning consonant sound given by the teacher to choose the right word. (5) Associating letter sounds and forms so that when the pupil sees the letter form, he thinks at once of the sound. (6) Using spoken context and the seen beginning letter to determine the proper word. (7) Using the context spoken by the teacher and the undetermined printed word seen by the pupil who, recognizing the initial consonant, may speak the word correctly. Later, the pupil will be taught also to use some of the additional letters and groups of letters in recognizing the word.

After the teaching procedures outlined above were completed, additional instruction was given. Several more consonant letter-sound associations were taught and used to identify words when the spoken context was given. Fourteen service words that make up one-fourth of printed English were taught. Then, near the end of the year, pupils read preprimers and perhaps parts of basal readers used in their school.

Adjustments in the teaching of reading were made for these pupils during their first five grades in school. In grade one, teaching the letter-sound associations already learned in kindergarten and use of the preprimers already read were omitted. Endings, such as *-ing, -ed, -ly,* and *-est* and their use were taught. Letter-sound associations for vowels used as initial letters in words were introduced. A primer or material in a first reader, whichever came directly after what had been read in kindergarten, was used in printed context, or the context was read aloud by the teacher. Pupils were trained to use initial consonants and additional sounds only as needed to identify a word. Suitable supplementary books were given to pupils to read on their own.

Early in the second and third grades, letter-sound associations for vowels not yet learned were taught. And letter-sound associations for common syllables were introduced and used with context as an aid. Pupils in second grade were started with books not used in grade one. New words appearing in a unit were taught before reading the selection. Again, suitable supplementary books were used. Detailed materials were provided and instruction given for preparation for reading in the social studies. In the third grade, further emphasis was placed upon use of context. The dictionary was used to get the meaning of new words. The pupils were also taught to interpret simple unfamiliar metaphors and to give proper attention to punctuation.

Special adjustments were also made for these pupils when they reached the fourth and fifth grades. The letter-sound associations taught in kindergarten, first, and second grades were checked. Deficiencies were remedied. Teachers were provided with detailed suggestions for helping improve the skills needed by pupils to overcome the particular difficulties they met in their reading. Pupils used basal readers that came next in the series after those they had finished reading in the previous grade.

New words were introduced to them prior to reading a unit. Suggestions for teaching pupils skills needed in reading informative materials were given to the teachers, such as the use of an index, locating the topic sentence, adjusting rate of reading to the purpose of the reading, outlining, and interpreting graphs. Special instructions were given for teaching social studies and other informative materials. Pupils were encouraged to use skills learned previously and were taught how to employ reference books. Instruction was given on organizing information gained from one or more sources. Planned discussions were carried out. Individualized reading was fostered by suggestions by the teacher. Oral reading was done by both pupils and teacher.

In addition to the kindergarten groups assigned to the experimental program outlined above, a control group was taught with materials and methods ordinarily used in the Denver schools. The main purpose in the control group was to develop reading readiness. (See chapters on preschool children.) Then, in the intermediate grades, emphasis was placed upon improving speed and comprehension, use of reference books, the mastery of specialized reading skills, and word analysis. In grades one through five, appropriate basal readers plus supplementary reading materials were used. This program was similar to that followed in many schools throughout the country. In contrast, the experimental program provided for early, sequential development in the kindergarten of skills basic to reading to be followed by an adjusted and accelerated program in the grades. It was found that in the later grades, progress in reading was faster in the experimental than in the control group.

The entire experimental design provided for four groups: (1) Control Group I had the regular kindergarten and the regular reading program in grades one through five. (2) Group II had the regular kindergarten program but an experimentally adjusted program through the first five grades. (3) Group III had the experimental program in kindergarten but the regular reading program in grades one through five. (4) Group IV had the experimental program in kindergarten and the adjusted experimental procedures in grades one through five.

Evaluation of progress in reading in each of these groups was made periodically throughout the period of experiment, that is, from kindergarten through the first five grades. Standardized and informal tests were used. Elaborate statistical analyses were made to compare the progress of the four groups in an attempt to determine the long-range effectiveness of teaching reading in kindergarten, as reflected at the end of grades one, three, and five. A summary of the results of the experiment follows.

The kindergarten pupils in the experimental program did learn certain beginning reading skills. Also, they lost relatively little of what they had learned over the summer vacation. And the learning of reading skills was distributed over the entire kindergarten year. During the last six weeks of kindergarten, *some* of the pupils were to read preprimers and primers. Most were able to recognize letters and letter sounds and with the help of verbal context could read certain words.

At the end of first grade, Group I, which had had regular kindergarten and regular first-grade instruction, was lower in reading achievement than the other three groups, while experimental Group IV which had received experimental instruction in kindergarten and adjusted instruction in grade one was significantly higher than the other groups. Both Group II, with regular kindergarten followed by adjusted instruction in grade one, and Group III, which received reading instruction in kindergarten and then were in the regular first-grade program, were better readers at the end of grade one than the control Group I. In all groups, girls did better than boys. There was an appreciable relationship between reading achievement and mental maturity.

The experimental group, which had reading instruction in kindergarten folowed by the adjusted, accelerated program in grades one through five, did significantly better than Group III which had the kindergarten reading instruction but the regular reading program through the grades. Effects of the initial start in reading in the kindergarten were lost in Group III by the end of second grade. This indicates that to maintain early gains, instruction needs to be adjusted in the grades. The experimental group also did better than Group II which had not started reading in kindergarten but had been in an adjusted program in grade one and on through grade five. This suggests the importance of starting reading in kindergarten. But Group II did better than those in the control Group I. They also did better than the Group III pupils who had reading in kindergarten and regular instruction thereafter. Evaluation showed that the experimental group excelled in their knowledge of word meanings over all other groups in grades three and five. The same held true for paragraph comprehension and rate of reading.

The conclusions are: Reading instruction in the kindergarten resulted in higher levels of reading achievement through grade five, except for Group III. But the maximum gains were achieved only when the program in the grades was adjusted to capitalize on achievement in the kindergarten. Otherwise, the gains disappeared by the end of the second grade. Although some of the kindergarten children learned to read, others did not progress that far. And when, after regular kindergarten, pupils beginning first grade were given the same program as used with the group in the experimental kindergarten followed by the adjusted accelerated instruction through grade five, they were next to the experimental group in achievement.

In evaluating the results of this study, it should be kept in mind that during the kindergarten year only about twenty minutes a day were spent in reading instruction. The rest of the time was devoted to the usual development of readiness for reading. Note also that marked individual differences occurred in the achievement of reading skills. And only during the last six weeks of the kindergarten year was actual reading done. No harmful effects of teaching reading in kindergarten appeared. Visual function was not impaired. And no more children were retarded in reading than in the control group. No evidence appeared that personality was adversely affected.

Actually, a large part of the experimental kindergarten program was devoted to getting ready to read, as described by McKee and Harrison. These activities included using spoken context, distinguishing letter forms from one another, listening for beginning sounds in words, associating letter sounds and forms, using spoken context and letter-sound associations, and using spoken context and the first letter of a printed word. As indicated in Chapter 11, some program of this sort should be used in all modern kindergartens. Any such program to be successful must be competently organized and provide for adjustment to individual differences. It is noteworthy that Group II, the delayed experimental group which received in grade one the same experimental program as Group IV had in the kindergarten, that is, the getting-ready-to-read program of McKee and Harrison, followed by reading, were next to the experimental group in reading achievement by the end of grade five. Obviously, the getting-ready-to-read program, whether given in kindergarten or grade one, is effective in promoting development in reading. For those pupils in kindergarten who do well in this program, opportunity should be provided to do some reading near the end of the year. When the McKee and Harrison program is used in combination with the program for kindergarten outlined in Chapter 11, many pupils will then be ready to start reading. Probably there would be little difference in results whether the reading of texts was begun during the last six weeks of kindergarten or not until the beginning of grade one. However, beginning to read before leaving kindergarten may give pupils a stimulating sense of achievement which will add to their eagerness to enter first grade. In any case, a number of pupils in most any kindergarten will continue to need experiences basic to reading, as outlined in Chapter 11.

In general, it may be concluded that some, but not all, children early in the kindergarten year will be ready for the type of program described above as reading but really consisting chiefly of preparation for reading. Actual reading can then begin near the end of kindergarten or at the start of grade one. From then on into succeeding grades, the reading program will need to be adjusted to include appropriate review of what has already been learned, teaching of new material by methods to which the pupils have already become accustomed, whenever this is practicable, and acceleration for those pupils who are ready to proceed at a more rapid pace. Every pupil should be permitted and encouraged to advance as rapidly as his skills allow at each grade level.

It should be kept in mind that reading readiness should be continued along with the reading program, grade by grade as needed. No kindergarten or preschool program can prepare a child adequately for reading new units, as he advances up through the grades. This has been noted in Chapter 11.

Chapter 13.
The Teacher, the Parent, and the Child

Teacher, parent, and child are all three involved in the educational process by which the child learns to read. The parent sets the stage during the preschool years by getting to know his child, teaching him various skills, awakening his interest in the world around him, introducing him to the pleasures to be found in books, and giving him the love and security which enable him to develop self-reliance and to relate happily to both children and adults.

In kindergarten, the teacher will soon find that your child has a personality all his own. Whatever his natural aptitudes, they have been shaped by five years of living and learning. He has developed habits of behavior and attitudes toward himself and others which will tend to persist. Also, he has acquired certain skills and interests and some factual knowledge. Probably he has not learned what it is like to work and play in a large group of children of his own age. While this may present no problem in the kindergarten situation which is so new to him, it will not be surprising if at first he is timid or overly aggressive, depending upon his personality. Or he may show his uneasiness by lack of persistence when all that is going on distracts him from whatever he is supposed to be doing. The teacher would then like to know whether he is just reacting to the new and strange situation or whether his unacceptable behavior is of a long-standing nature. Very likely the parents are beginning to wonder why their child does not seem to like kindergarten even though he went with eager anticipation on the first day. And the child himself knows that he is not very happy and may be somewhat bewildered by his discomfort and the disapproval he often feels directed toward him.

This is one kind of situation illustrating the triple involvement of teacher, pupil, and parent in whatever goes on in the child's educational experience. Many others are more directly concerned with the teaching and learning of specific skills and subject matter. Almost always the child's progress is more rapid and any problems he may encounter are solved more easily when teacher, parent, and child work together. In learning to read, the child will gain from much more practice than is possible during the school day. But the parents must know what and how he is being taught so that their efforts will mesh smoothly with what the teacher is having him do at school. The teacher will be glad to explain to the parents how they can supplement her efforts. She will also advise as to what books are suitable for the parents to use in reading aloud to their child. There may be still other ways in which parents can fill in any gaps the teacher notes in the child's preparation for work in the primary grades, such as by placing more emphasis at home on his working independently, seeking more opportunities for him to play with other children, or widening his experience with more trips to nearby places.

Schools have sometimes been slow to recognize the essential role of the parents in educating their child. But educators are becoming increasingly aware that teachers need the informed assistance of the parents. This awareness is indicated in a group of articles in *The Reading Teacher*, May 1970, all of which stress that parents and teacher must be partners if the teaching of reading is to be truly successful. And this partnership should be continued at least through the elementary grades.

To work together effectively, each must know what the other is doing. Schools have a responsibility to acquaint parents with the school program, its goals, and its methods. Parents are equally obligated to share with the teacher whatever information she needs as to the child's health, behavior at home, and attitudes expressed at home about school. Also, it will be helpful to the teacher to be given at least a general idea of the home situation. Some schools now arrange special study and discussion groups for all parents whose children are in the same grade. With filmstrips and explanations, the teacher acquaints them with what she is attempting to teach her pupils and how she goes about doing it. She then invites their questions and comments. At such meetings, parents also benefit from the opportunity to talk with each other about their part in supplementing the school program with activities at home and about any problems of mutual interest relating to their children's school experience. Parent-teacher associations may be instrumental in promoting meetings of this sort.

In the primary grades, the teacher uses many devices to prepare her pupils for a new reading unit. The teacher's manuals which accompany a series of readers give specific suggestions on preparation for reading a new story. Steps taken in doing this usually include the following:

1. The new vocabulary is presented. The words are usually written on the chalkboard, sometimes in brief sentences so that the context will help in learning each new word. Another method is to present the new word with others familiar to the pupil that rhyme with it and to ask him to note the differences in beginning sounds. The names of the characters in the story are talked about. Also, phonetic clues are given to help in identifying new words. Action words may be dramatized to make them more meaningful.

2. The purpose of the reading to be done is clearly indicated. Examining and discussing the picture or

pictures that accompany a story will help the pupils to infer what it is all about and what may happen. Also, the teacher can explain in a general way the nature of the story or factual unit. She can then raise a few questions to stimulate a search for answers. If the text is appropriate, the pupils can be asked a question at each new page or section to aid them in focusing their attention upon whatever is of prime importance in what they are reading.

3. Sometimes the story is such that rereading it aloud is interesting. Stories with conversation between different characters lend themselves to assigning a child to each character and one or more others to read the parts that are not conversational.

4. There are various ways to provide practice in determining the main idea of parts of the story and of the story as a whole. Pairs of children may work on this together and the conclusions reached can be written in sentences on the chalkboard for further comparison. Or the main idea can be sought by general class discussion.

5. Most stories provide opportunity for practice in using word-recognition techniques, such as use of word form (configuration), phonetic analysis, structural analysis, or determining the word from the context.

6. Ordinarily when a story is finished, it is discussed by members of the class and the teacher. It may be compared with other stories which preceded it and amplified by reports of individual pupils or their teacher of related experiences or supplementary factual information.

7. The teacher may then read aloud a similar story and invite comparisons between the two.

As a parent, you can borrow devices such as these and adapt them for use in informal reading situations with your child at home. Take the story of *The Hare and the Tortoise,* no doubt familiar to you from your own childhood. Perhaps your child has chosen this new story to read with you because of his interest in the pictures accompanying it in which he sees a rabbit and a turtle. He thinks that the rabbit is bigger than the ones he has seen and tells you that a friend of his now has a baby turtle. You recall to him the huge turtle you both saw at the zoo. You now introduce him to the new words *hare* and *tortoise* and perhaps print the words *rabbit* and *turtle* and let him compare them with the new ones. He will find that *tortoise* and *turtle* both start with the same letter but otherwise are different and that *rabbit* and *hare* have no common beginning or ending. Then you might explain (even if you have to first consult the dictionary) that a hare is bigger than a rabbit and that a tortoise is a turtle that lives on dry land while some kinds of turtles prefer the water. Looking quickly through the story, you may find a few other words to clear up in advance so that the reading can proceed more smoothly, such as *swift* as applied to the hare and *plodding* used to describe the turtle's slow movements. Identify these words for your child, if he does not already know them, and associate them with words he does know, such as *fast* and *slow*. You can also tell him, if he has not already found out from the pictures, that this is a story of a race between the tortoise and the hare, and ask which one he thinks will win. At appropriate places in the story, as your child pauses while reading it aloud, ask what he supposes will happen next or make similar inquiries or comments to stimulate his thinking about what the hare or the tortoise is doing or trying to do. After the story is finished, the two of you might talk about it somewhat as follows:

CHILD: The tortoise won after all.
MOTHER: But the hare ran faster.
CHILD: He took a nap.

MOTHER: Wasn't the tortoise tired, too?

CHILD: Well, he didn't run so fast.

MOTHER: He kept plodding along.

CHILD: That's why he won the race—he kept plodding along.

MOTHER: You're right. If you keep plodding along, you may win while others take time out to rest or to have fun.

CHILD: I like the tortoise.

On another day, if the storybook includes direct conversation between the hare and the tortoise, the two of you could reread it with your child taking the part of the tortoise while you read what the hare says, or vice versa.

In the primary grades, the teacher will periodically evaluate your child's abilities and progress in reading by the use of tests. She will undoubtedly confer with you about the tests results. These will be obtained from both standardized and informal, or teacher-made, tests. Very likely the first test will be for reading readiness, given near the end of the kindergarten year or during the first few weeks of grade one. One of the better of these tests is the *Metropolitan Readiness Tests* (Harcourt Brace Jovanovich). In giving this or any test, the teacher must be sure that each child understands the directions. Suggestions on interpreting the test results are given in the examiner's manual. The teacher can also consult C. M. McCullough's and my book, *Teaching Elementary Reading* (Appleton-Century-Crofts), for suggestions on interpretation of readiness test scores.

In grades one through three, the teacher will gain much information as to your child's progress in reading and about any difficulties he may be having by use of the informal tests. At the end of teaching each skill, such as mastery of initial consonants, phrasing (reading by thought units), vocabulary knowledge, comprehension, the teacher will make up an informal test to check how well each pupil has learned what has been taught. Tests that may be used as models for teacher-made tests are given in the manuals that accompany books in series of readers. Frequent tests of this kind enable her to give prompt help to any students who have not yet mastered any parts of the unit which has just been taught. By keeping individual test results in each child's cumulative folder, the teacher acquires an ongoing record of all the children in her room. As a supplement to test results, she keeps a record of her observations of pupil behavior and responses in the reading situation, such as high enthusiasm, moderate interest, or indifference, distaste, or anxiety. It is desirable to note initial reactions and whatever changes in attitude occur from time to time. Only by accumulating records of test scores and observations, together with anecdotal notes, can the teacher watch closely and accurately the progress of each of the children in her class.

In addition to the standardized tests used to evaluate reading readiness are others that measure progress in reading. Reading achievement tests are ordinarily given at the beginning of the school year, starting with the second grade, and may be repeated at the end of a term or year. Lists of reading achievement tests are given in the Appendix of *Teaching Elementary Reading*. The tests used by the teacher should be selected to measure what she has been teaching. The teacher or administrator should examine sample copies of tests and carefully read the examiner's manual before ordering in quantity for a class. There are many tests designed for use in each of the primary grades. They cover vocabulary, comprehension, word recognition, and other aspects of reading. When using a standardized test, it is imperative that the directions that accompany it be followed exactly. Otherwise, the standardized norms which indicate the reading level of the pupil are useless.

Standardized tests provide an essential method of appraising the reading level a pupil has reached. They are measuring devices of proved reliability and validity. Also they are readily scored, and the scores are easily interpreted by consulting the manual of directions. A reliable test is one that yields consistent performance when the test, or an equivalent form, is given a short time after it is first given. This means that a child achieves about the same score on repetition of the test. A valid test is one that yields a true and accurate measure of the aspect of reading for which it was constructed, such as comprehension of paragraphs. Norms or standards for a test are established by giving the test to a sufficiently large and representative group of pupils. Mean, or average, scores are computed for successive grade levels and then are listed in tabular form in the examiner's manual. When such a test is given, the teacher can refer to the averages to find out the grade level obtained by each pupil in her class. Thus, strengths and weaknesses of a pupil can be discovered in various aspects of reading achievement, such as vocabulary knowledge, speed of reading, and skill in word recognition. The teacher must keep in mind that the norms are averages and that some pupils will be above and others below the average for her class. Such deviations are to be expected. Should too many of her pupils score below the norm, the teacher is challenged to reconsider the methods of instruction she has been using.

Although only those who prepare achievement tests and those who use them are concerned with their details, parents may appreciate knowing what they are and what purposes they serve. This may be especially true for parents who otherwise may confuse them with tests of intelligence or may wonder why their child who is only in the primary grades so often speaks of having tests at school. As a matter of fact, many children do not distinguish achievement tests from other exercises the teacher gives them to do. The main usefulness of the test scores on informal and standardized tests is for guidance in adapting instruction to the individual needs of the pupil. The manual of directions supplied with the test forms usually gives suggestions for using the test results for diagnostic and remedial procedures with pupils who need additional help.

It is evident that the teacher is experienced in the selection and use of many techniques not familiar to most parents for teaching children to read. But there is nothing mysterious about her methods and it is to the advantage of parent, teacher, and child for parents to acquire a general understanding of how reading is being taught. Of similar importance is the teacher's understanding of the child's background and present home situation. The child is fortunate who has devoted parents and a teacher who inspires his confidence and knows how best to teach him. But unless parents and teacher coordinate their efforts, the child is the loser. When your child complains about something that happened at school, you can handle his complaint more wisely if you are already acquainted with his teacher. Likewise, it is much easier for the teacher to meet any problem that may arise with your child when she knows she can count on your support and cooperation.

Many parents find activities with their children from six to nine somewhat easier and sometimes more enjoyable than during the preschool years. When their child can already read simple material, both parent and child will find much pleasure in his reading aloud. There are many ways in which you can help him improve his reading skills, such as encouraging him to find rhyming words in poems and to think up others of his own, providing additional practice in identifying beginning and ending sounds of words, discriminating sounds that are alike or different, and thinking up synonyms for words, such as *fast* for *swift*. Your child's range of interest in stories which he can read or you can read to him has widened and he comes forth with more ideas of his own about what he reads or hears. Frequent trips with him to the public library will insure ample reading material, some of which he will delight in choosing for himself. His questions about what he learns from books or other experiences are becoming ever more challenging and may even require his parents to do some reading on their own to answer them to his satisfaction. When the answer is rather lengthy, his attention does not wander as it would have before he went to school. His reports on what he learns at school and what happens there include many more details than when he attended kindergarten. Many tasks around home which earlier were too difficult for him he now does with ease and satisfaction. He has made friends at school, and activities with them on the school playground and in the neighborhood have become an important part of his life. Probably he is developing some special interests, such as collecting shells, hunting for lizards, or learning to swim and is proud of his accomplishments in such activities. And he is ready and eager for more extensive exploration of places of interest previously visited or new to him. What he observes and what he thinks about his experiences often astonish and delight his parents. Building upon sound teaching and training in his preschool years, his education at home and at school can now proceed at a rapid pace.

Chapter 14.
Concluding Summary

Experience and experimental evidence show that the child who is properly prepared for reading will learn well when he is given reading instruction. Activities that help prepare a child for reading begin as early as two years of age, and perhaps somewhat earlier for some children. Parents can provide their child with the experiences he needs to be ready for reading in first grade, or perhaps in kindergarten. No expensive equipment will be required, as everyday activities in the home and neighborhood, together with planned trips to nearby places of interest to the child and family excursions, make excellent teaching material for the young child if properly utilized by his parents. A few picture books, storybooks to be read aloud to him, and the usual toys and crayons will be about all else that is needed.

It is essential that these experiences be appropriate to the maturity level of the child. This means that activities should be selected that the child is ready for *now*. That is, the parents should make frequent informal evaluations of their child's maturity, his interests, motor skills, and prior experiences. Only then can they judge what their child can do satisfactorily at different levels of development, whether at two years of age or at successive ages. Numerous everyday experiences in the home that are valuable for preparing your child for reading have been discussed in Chapter 4. Parents are not only the first teachers of their child but are likely to be the most important ones he will ever have. Through well-chosen experiences outside the home your child will learn to adjust to other children and will overcome any undue shyness with adults. And he will become more and more acquainted with the world around him.

Parents always want their child to feel secure and happy, to have self-respect and respect for others. To this end, good communication between parent and child is essential. Parents who get to know their child well enough to understand and appreciate his feelings as well as his abilities will have little trouble in maintaining a good rapport with him. A child responds well to parents whose love and respect he is sure of and who find time to enjoy activities with him. Under such favorable circumstances he becomes eager to learn new skills and to win parental aproval. His efforts as well as his accomplishments merit full appreciation and recognition. When success is not immediate, persistence should be encouraged. Discipline should be maintained where needed and permissiveness whenever appropriate. All parents make mistakes at times but, if the parent-child relationship is sound, these can be corrected without undue difficulty.

Healthy growth in both physical and mental abilities are dependent to a considerable extent upon parental care. A healthy, happy, and alert child stands a good chance of adjusting well to the entire school situation. Parents should watch out for any physical handicap as their child is developing in the preschool years and later. A few children have hearing and vision difficulties even at early ages. Various signs of these handicaps are described and discussed in Chapter 9. Competent professional help whenever such signs are noted may make correction possible before the child enters school. If a child's handicap cannot be corrected, parents and teachers can help him adjust to it.

Book experience for your child should begin early and be continued without interruption through the years that follow. Even the two-year-old enjoys looking at picture books designed for the very young child, especially if he is sitting on his mother's lap and she talks with him about what he sees. Gradually, with guidance, your child will learn to "read," that is, interpret, pictures. A series of pictures that tell a story are particularly enjoyed, as outlined in Chapter 10. Read stories and verses to your child. As he grows older they will hold his attention for longer and longer periods of time, and he will discover the pleasure to be derived from books. Conversation about what is read, including questions asked and answered, will aid in vocabulary development, verbal facility, and comprehension, all of which are basic to preparation for learning to read.

The ability to distinguish objects visually begins at an early age and develops rather rapidly as the child grows older, especially if the parents give some guidance. At first, the child makes only overall discriminations (chair, baby, spoon). As he reaches four and five years of age he can be guided to make such fine discriminations as variations in the forms of letters and words. This is discussed in Chapter 8. He will need this ability as he starts to learn to read. Auditory discrimination can also be encouraged and developed from an early age. The very young child distinguishes the sounds of footsteps, running water, a barking dog, and the like. Later, he will be able to tell the difference between high- or low-pitched sounds, those that are long or short, and harsh or soft. When your child reaches about five years of age, he can be taught to discriminate between the sounds of different letters of the alphabet. He will need this skill to determine the sounds of letters in words as he begins to read. (See Chapter 7.)

When your child enters kindergarten at about five years of age, get acquainted with the kindergarten program and with his teacher. She will welcome your help in understanding your child and meeting his needs. Be ready to listen appreciatively to whatever your child wants to tell you about each kindergarten day. Keep in touch with his progress at school and learn from the teacher what you can do at home to supplement his kindergarten activities, particularly those providing preparation for reading. The modern kindergarten does not eliminate the child's contact with written words. (See Chapters 11 and 12.) Some reading may be taught those children who are ready for reading instruction. In any case, your child will be ready to learn the letters of the alphabet and certain words, such as his name, names of objects in the schoolroom, and traffic signs, if he does not know them already. For the average child, the kindergarten period is primarily for further preparation for reading. This preparation occurs both at school and at home.

Throughout the kindergarten and the primary grades, the teacher, the parent, and the child work together as a team to promote the child's adjustment to school and to foster progress in reading. The concerned and interested parent will strive for a good working relationship with the teacher and her child during kindergarten and the primary grades. Expanded and guided activities outside the school will help your child to progress more rapidly in his reading.

A few children are reading before they enter kindergarten. School facilities should be provided so that they can continue these reading activities. Some others will be ready to start reading when they arrive at kindergarten. To the extent that the kindergarten program permits, they should receive reading instruction. The methods and materials used in teaching reading at the kindergarten level should not be the same as those used in grade one. (See Chapters 11 and 12.) A number of kindergarten children will not be ready for reading instruction. They should have a readiness program as outlined in Chapter 11.

Children in the primary grades will need and profit by certain readiness activities. A few children are not yet ready for the regular reading program upon entering grade one. They should have a continuation of the kindergarten program until they are ready. After children begin reading, they still need preparation for each new unit of reading, as described in Chapter 13.

In conclusion, it is safe to say that the child who is well prepared for reading, as discussed in the earlier chapters of this book, will receive reading instruction with eagerness and with a good chance of success. Adequate reading performance will bring him much happiness and motivate him for continued success in his schoolwork.

Appendix A
Books to Read Together

PRESCHOOL AND KINDERGARTEN*

A is for Alphabet. Glenview, Illinois: Scott, Foresman & Co., 1968.

Alexander, Martha, *Out! Out! Out!* New York: The Dial Press, 1968.

Anglund, Joan W., *Brave Cowboy*. New York: Harcourt, Brace & World, 1959.

Anglund, Joan W., *In a Pumpkin Shell: A Mother Goose ABC*. New York: Harcourt, Brace & World, 1960.

Appell, Clara and Morey, *Now I have a Daddy Haircut*. New York: Dodd, Mead & Co., 1969.

Balet, Jan B., *The Gift, A Portuguese Christmas Tale*. New York: The Delacorte Press, 1967.

Beim, Jerrold, *Andy and the School Bus*. New York: William Morrow and Co., Inc., 1947.

Beim, Jerrold, *The Smallest Boy in the Class*. New York: William Morrow and Co., Inc., 1949.

Beim, Jerrold, *Too Many Sisters*. New York: William Morrow and Co., Inc., 1956.

Bemelmans, Ludwig, *Madeline in London*. New York: The Viking Press, Inc., 1961.

Bendick, Jeanne, *What Could You See?* New York: McGraw-Hill Inc., 1957.

Blough, Glenn O., *After the Sun Goes Down*. New York: McGraw-Hill Inc., 1956.

Book of Nursery and Mother Goose Rhymes, Illustrated by Marguerite de Angeli. New York: Doubleday & Co., Inc., 1966.

Burningham, John, *ABC*. Indianapolis: The Bobbs-Merrill Co., Inc., 1967.

Burton, Virginia Lee, *Little House*. Boston: Houghton Mifflin Co.

Carle, Eric, *One, Two, Three to the Zoo*. New York: Harcourt, Brace & World, 1968.

*Many of these books and many other suitable ones can be borrowed from the public library.

Carroll, Ruth (Robinson), *The Chimp and the Clown*. New York: Henry Z. Walck, Inc., 1968.

Carroll, Ruth and Latrobe, *Where's the Bunny?* New York: Oxford University Press, 1950.

Carter, Katharine J., *Hoppy Long Legs*. Austin, Texas: Steck-Vaughn, 1963.

Chalmers, Mary, *Be Good, Harry*. New York: Harper & Row, Publishers, 1967.

Chicken Little, Henny Penny. New York: The Seabury Press, 1968.

Cohen, Miriam, *Will I Have a Friend?* New York: The Macmillan Co., 1967.

Duvoisin, Roger, *Petunia*. New York: Alfred A. Knopf, Inc., 1950.

Emberley, Barbara, *Drummer Hoff*. Englewood Cliffs, New Jersey: Prentice-Hall, Inc., 1967.

Ets, Marie Hall, *Gilberto and the Wind*. New York: The Viking Press, Inc., 1963.

Ets, Marie Hall, *Talking Without Words*. New York: The Viking Press, Inc., 1968.

Fatio, Louise, *The Happy Lion*. New York: Whittlesey House, 1954.

Fontane, Theodor, *Sir Ribbeck of Ribbeck of Havelland*. New York: The Macmillan Co., 1969.

Foster, Joanna, *Pete's Puddle*. New York: Harcourt, Brace & World, 1969.

Françoise, *The Thank-You Book*. New York: Charles Scribner's Sons, 1947.

Freeman, Don, *Corduroy*. New York: The Viking Press, Inc., 1968.

Friskey, Margaret, *Chicken Little, Count-to-Ten*. Chicago: Children's Press, 1946.

Galdone, Paul, *The Hare and the Tortoise*. New York: McGraw-Hill Inc., 1962.

Galdone, Paul, *The Old Woman and Her Pig*. New York: McGraw-Hill Inc.

Gay, Zhenya, *The Nicest Time of the Year*. New York: The Viking Press, Inc., 1960.

Goodall, John S., *The Adventures of Paddy Pork*. New York: Harcourt, Brace & World, 1968.

Gramatky, Hardie, *Little Toot*. New York: G. P. Putnam's Sons, 1939.

Grifalconi, Ann, *The Toy Trumpet*. Indianapolis: The Bobbs-Merrill Co., Inc., 1968.

Hader, Berta and Elmer, *The Big Snow*. New York: The Macmillan Co.

Hawkinson, John and Hawkinson, Lucy (Ozone), *Little Boy Who Lives Up High*. Chicago: Albert Whitman and Co., 1967.

Hewett, Anita, *Mrs. Mopple's Washing Line*. New York: McGraw-Hill Inc., 1966.

Higgins, Loyta, *Stop* and *Go*. New York: Simon and Schuster, Inc.

Humphreys, Dena, *Animals Every Child Should Know*. New York: Grosset & Dunlap, Inc., 1962.

Hush Little Baby: A Folk Lullaby. Englewood Cliffs, New Jersey: Prentice-Hall, Inc., 1968.

Johnson, La Verne, *Night Noises*. New York: Parents' Magazine Press, 1968.

Keats, Ezra J., *The Little Drummer Boy*. New York: The Macmillan Co., 1968.

Keats, Ezra J., *The Snowy Day*. New York: The Viking Press, Inc., 1962.

Keats, Ezra J., *Whistle for Willie*. New York: The Viking Press, Inc., 1969.

Kimball, Sabra and Heathcote, *The Doubleday First Guide to Birds*. Garden City, New York: Doubleday & Co., Inc., 1963.

Kishida, Eriko, *The Hippo Boat*. New York: Harcourt, Brace & World, 1968.

Krauss, Ruth, *A Hole Is to Dig*. New York: Harper & Row, Publishers, 1952.

Kroeber, Theodora, *A Green Christmas*. Berkeley, California: Parnassus Press, 1967.

Langstaff, John, and Rojankovsky, Feodor, *Frog Went A-Courtin*. New York: Harcourt, Brace & World, 1955.

Leaf, Munro, *Boo, Who Used to Be Scared of the Dark*. New York: Random House, Inc.

Lenski, Lois, *Let's Play House*. New York: Henry Z. Walck, Inc., 1944.

Lenski, Lois, *The Little Fire Engine*. New York: Henry Z. Walck, Inc., 1956.

Lenski, Lois, *Papa Small*. New York: Henry Z. Walck, Inc., 1963.

Lenski, Lois, *We Live in the City*. Philadelphia: J. B. Lippincott Co., 1954.

Lexau, Joan M., *Every Day a Dragon*. New York: Harper & Row, Publishers, 1967.

MacDonald, Golden, *Red Light, Green Light*. Garden City, New York: Doubleday & Co., Inc., 1944.

McCloskey, Robert, *Make Way for Ducklings*. New York: The Viking Press, Inc., 1941.

Mendoza, George, *The Scarecrow Clock*. New York: Holt, Rinehart and Winston, 1971.

Milgrom, Harry, *Adventures with a Paper Cup*. New York: E. P. Dutton and Co., 1968.

Milgrom, Harry, *Adventures with a Paper Plate*. New York: E. P. Dutton and Co., 1968.

Mills, Alan and Boone, Rose, *I Know an Old Lady*. Skokie, Illinois: Rand McNally & Co., 1961.

Mother Goose: The Comic Adventures of Old Mother Hubbard and her Dog. Englewood Cliffs, New Jersey: Bradbury Press, 1968.

Munari, Bruno, *Bruno Munari's ABC*. New York: Harcourt, Brace & World, 1960.

Munari, Bruno, *Bruno Munari's Zoo*. New York: Harcourt, Brace & World, 1963.

Munari, Bruno, *Jimmy Has Lost His Cap*. New York: Harcourt, Brace & World, 1959.

Myers, Bernice, *Not This Bear*. New York: Four Winds Press, Scholastic Magazines, Inc., 1968.

Neurath, Marie, *Too Small to See*. New York: Sterling Publishing Co., 1957.

Olschewski, Alfred, *The Wheel Rolls Over*. Boston: Little, Brown and Co., 1962.

Oxenbury, Helen, *Numbers of Things*. New York: Franklin Watts, Inc., 1967.

Peppé, Rodney, *The Alphabet Book*. New York: Four Winds Press, Scholastic Magazine, Inc., 1968.

Petersham, Maud and Miski, *Off to Bed*. New York: Simon and Schuster, Inc., 1961.

Preston, Edna Mitchell, *Monkey in the Jungle*. New York: The Viking Press, Inc., 1968.

Provensen, Alice and Provensen, Martin, *What Is Color?* New York: Golden Press, 1967.

Ressner, Philip, *At Night*. New York: E. P. Dutton and Co., 1967.

Scott, Ann H., *Sam*. New York: McGraw-Hill Inc., 1967.

Skorpen, Liesel M., *Outside My Window*. New York: Harper & Row, Publishers, 1968.

Schmiderer, Dorothy, *The Alphabeast Book: An Abecedarium*. New York: Holt, Rinehart and Winston, 1971.

Tresselt, Alvin, *Frog in the Well*. New York: Lothrop, Lee & Shepard Co., 1958.

Tresselt, Alvin, *Rain Drop Splash*. New York: Lothrop, Lee & Shepard Co.

Tresselt, Alvin, *White Snow, Bright Snow*. New York: Lothrop, Lee & Shepard Co.

Van Leeuwen, Jean, *Timothy's Flower*. New York: Random House, Inc., 1967.

Waber, Bernard, *An Anteater Named Arthur*. Boston: Houghton Mifflin Co., 1967.

Wildsmith, Brian, *Brian Wildsmith's ABC*. New York: Franklin Watts, Inc., 1963.

Wildsmith, Brian, *Brian Wildsmith's Wild Animals*. New York: Franklin Watts, Inc., 1967.

Williams, Gweneira, *Timid Timothy*. Glenview, Illinois: Scott, Foresman & Co., 1944.

Wondriska, William, *Mr. Brown and Mr. Gray*. New York: Holt, Rinehart and Winston, 1968.

Wright, Blanche F., *The Real Mother Goose*. Skokie, Illinois: Rand McNally & Co.

Yamaguchi, Marianne, *Finger Plays*. New York: Holt, Rinehart and Winston, 1970.

Zion, Gene, *The Dirty Dog*. New York: Harper & Row, Publishers, 1956.

BOOKS FOR GRADES ONE TO THREE[*]

Agle, Nan H., and Wilson, Ellen J. (Cameron), *Three Boys and H_2O*. New York: Charles Scribner's Sons, 1968.

Agle, Nan H., and Wilson, Ellen J., *Three Boys and Space*. New York: Charles Scribner's Sons, 1962.

Alain, *Elephant and the Flea*. New York: McGraw-Hill Inc., 1956.

[*] These can be read aloud also. Many of them and other suitable books can be found in the public library.

Alger, Leclaire, *Kellyburn Braes*. New York: Holt, Rinehart and Winston, 1968.

Alger, Leclaire, *The Laird of Cockpen*. New York: Holt, Rinehart and Winston, 1969.

And so my Garden Grows. New York: Doubleday & Co., Inc., 1969.

Anderson, Clarence W., *Blaze and the Gray Spotted Pony*. New York: The Macmillan Co., 1968.

Anderson, John L., and Adams, Adrienne, *Two Hundred Rabbits*. New York: The Viking Press, Inc., 1968.

Ardizzone, Edward, *Tim to the Lighthouse*. New York: Henry Z. Walck, 1968.

Ardizzone, Edward and Ardizzone, Aingelda, *The Little Girl and the Tiny Doll*. New York: The Delacorte Press, 1967.

Association for Childhood Education International, *Told Under the Blue Umbrella*. New York: The Macmillan Co., 1962.

Banner, Angella, *Aunt and Bee and ABC*. New York: Franklin Watts, 1967.

Baum, L. Frank, *Wizard of Oz*. New York: Random House, Inc., 1964.

Benchley, Nathaniel, *A Ghost Named Fred*. New York: Harper & Row, Publishers, 1968.

Bialk, Eliza, *Tizz in Cactus Country*. Chicago: Children's Press, 1964.

Branley, Franklyn M., *A Book of Mars for You*. New York: Crowell-Collier Press, 1968.

Brecht, Edith, *The Little Fox*. Philadelphia: J. B. Lippincott Co., 1968.

Bridwell, Norman, *Clifford, the Big Red Dog*. New York: Four Winds Press, Scholastic Magazines, Inc., 1966.

Brooke, Leslie L., *Johnny Crow's Garden*. New York: Frederick Warne and Co., 1903.

Brooke, Leslie L., *Johnny Crow's Party*. New York: Frederick Warne and Co., 1907.

Brown, Marcia, *How Hippo*. New York: Charles Scribner's Sons, 1969.

Brown, Marcia, *The Neighbors*. New York: Charles Scribner's Sons, 1967.

Brown, Margaret, *Golden Bunny*. Racine, Wisconsin: Western Publishing Co., 1953.

Buchheimer, Naomi, *Let's Go to a Bakery*. New York: G. P. Putnam's Sons, 1956.

Buchheimer, Naomi, *Let's Go to the Library*. New York: G. P. Putnam's Sons, 1957.

Burch, Robert, *Joey's Cat*. New York: The Viking Press, Inc., 1969.

Burningham, John, *Cannonball Simp*. Indianapolis: The Bobbs-Merrill Co., Inc., 1967.

Burningham, John, *Harquin: The Fox Who Went Down to the Valley*. Indianapolis: The Bobbs-Merrill Co., Inc., 1968.

Caldecott, Randolph, *The Queen of Hearts*. New York: Frederick Warne and Co., 1881.

Caldecott, Randolph, *Hey Diddle Diddle and Other Funny Poems*. New York: Frederick Warne and Co., 1882.

Calhoun, Mary, *The Goblin Under the Stairs*. New York: William Morrow and Co., 1968.

Carrick, Carol, and Carrick, Donald, *Swamp Spring*. New York: The Macmillan Co., 1969.

Caudill, Rebecca, *A Pocketful of Cricket*. New York: Holt, Rinehart and Winston, 1964.

Caudill, Rebecca and Ayars, *Contrary Jenkins*. New York: Holt, Rinehart and Winston, 1969.

Clifton, Lucille, *Some of the Days of Everett Anderson*. New York: Holt, Rinehart and Winston, 1970.

Clymer, Eleanor, *Adventure of Walter*. New York: Atheneum Publishers, 1965.

Collier, James L., *Danny Goes to the Hospital*. New York: W. W. Norton and Co., 1970.

Conklin, Gladys (Plemon), *Lucky Ladybugs*. New York: Holiday House, 1968.

Cooper, Elizabeth K., *The Fish from Japan*. New York: Harcourt, Brace & World, 1969.

Courlauder, H., and Herzog, G., *The Cow-Tail Switch and Other African Stories*. New York: Holt, Rinehart and Winston, 1947.

Cruse, Laurence A., *A Village in Normandy*. Indianapolis: The Bobbs-Merrill Co., 1968.

Daudet, Alphonse, *The Brave Little Goat of Monseiur Séguin: A Picture Story from Provence*. New York: Harcourt, Brace & World, 1968.

Davis, Katherine Kenniscott, and others, *The Little Drummer Boy*. New York: The Macmillan Co., 1968.

Duvoisin, Roger, *Donkey-Donkey*. New York: Parents' Magazine Press, 1968.

Earle, Olive L., *Praying Mantis*. New York: William Morrow and Co., 1969.

Elkin, Benjamin, *The Wisest Man in the World: A Legend of Ancient Israel, Retold*. New York: Parents' Magazine Press, 1968.

Elkin, Benjamin, *Such is the Way of the World*. New York: Parents' Magazine Press, 1968.

Emberley, Ed., *Green Says Go*. Boston: Little, Brown and Co., 1968.

Ets, Marie H., *Bad Boy, Good Boy*. New York: Crowell-Collier Press, 1967.

Fenton, Edward, *Fierce John*. New York: Holt, Rinehart and Winston, 1969.

Feravolo, Rocco V., *Around the World in Ninety Minutes*. New York: Lothrop, Lee & Shepard Co., 1968.

Fisher, Aileen Lucia, *Sing, Little Mouse*. New York: Crowell-Collier Press, 1969.

Fisher, Aileen Lucia, *We Went Looking*. New York: Crowell-Collier Press, 1968.

Freeman, Mae (Blacker), *The Book of Magnets*. New York: Four Winds Press, 1968.

Fritz, Jean, *George Washington's Breakfast*. New York: Coward-McCann, 1969.

Gans, Roma, *Hummingbirds in the Garden*. New York: Crowell-Collier Press, 1969.

Garelick, May, *Look at the Moon*. New York: William R. Scott, 1969.

Garfield, Nancy, *The Tuesday Elephant*. New York: Crowell-Collier Press, 1968.

Gobhai, Mehli, *The Blue Jackal*. Englewood Cliffs, New Jersey: Prentice-Hall, Inc., 1968.

Goldin, Augusta R., *The Sunlit Sea*. New York: Crowell-Collier Press, 1968.

Grabianski, Janusz, *Birds*. New York: Franklin Watts, 1968.

Grabianski, Janusz, *Dogs*. New York: Franklin Watts, 1968.

Greenberg, Polly, *Oh Lord, I Wish I Was a Buzzard*. New York: The Macmillan Co., 1968.

Grimm, Jakob L. K. and Grimm, W. K., *Jorinda and Joringel*. New York: Charles Scribner's Sons, 1968.

Grimm, Jakob Ludwig Karl and Grimm, Wilhelm Karl, *Little Red Riding Hood*. New York: Harcourt, Brace & World, 1969.

Hall, Rosalys, *The Bright and Shining Breadboard*. New York: Lothrop, Lee & Shepard Co., 1969.

Hawes, Judy, *Why Frogs are Wet*. New York: Crowell-Collier Press, 1968.

Hess, Lilo, *The Curious Raccoons*. New York: Charles Scribner's Sons, 1968.

Hitte, Kathryn, *When Noodlehead Went to the Fair*. New York: Parents' Magazine Press, 1968.

Hoban, Russell, *A Birthday for Frances*. New York: Harper & Row, Publishers, 1968.

Holl, Adelaide, *The Remarkable Egg*. New York: Lothrop, Lee & Shepard Co., 1968.

Hutchins, Pat, *Tom and Sam*. New York: The Macmillan Co., 1968.

Kane, Henry Bugbee, *Four Seasons in the Woods*. New York: Alfred A. Knopf, Inc., 1968.

Kaye, Geraldine, *The Sea Monkey*. New York: Harcourt, Brace & World, 1968.

Keats, Ezra J., *A Letter to Amy*. New York: Harper & Row, Publishers, 1968.

Kirn, Ann, *Beeswax Catches a Thief*. New York: W. W. Norton and Co., 1968.

Kirn, Ann, *Let's Look at Tracks*. New York: G. P. Putnam's Sons, 1969.

Koffler, Camilla, *Whose Eye Am I?* New York: Harper & Row, Publishers, 1969.

Lawrence, James D., *Binky Brothers, Detectives*. New York: Harper & Row, Publishers, 1968.

Lear, Edward, *The Four Little Children Who Went Around the World*. New York: The Macmillan Co., 1968.

Lear, Edward, *The Scroobius Pip*. New York: Harper & Row, Publishers, 1968.

Levenson, Dorothy, *The Magic Carousel*. New York: Parents' Magazine Press, 1967.

Lexau, Joan M., *The Rooftop Mystery*. New York: Harper & Row, Publishers, 1968.

Lobel, Arnold, *The Great Blueness and Other Predicaments*. New York: Harper & Row, Publishers, 1968.

Matsutani, Miyoko, *The Crane Maiden*. New York: Parents' Magazine Press, 1968.

McGovern, Ann, *Too Much Noise*. Boston: Houghton Mifflin Co., 1967.

Miles, Miska, *Nobody's Cat*. Boston: Little, Brown and Co., 1969.

Monjo, F. N., *The Drinking Gourd*. New York: Harper & Row, Publishers, 1970.

Monjo, F. N., *Indian Summer*. New York: Harper & Row, Publishers, 1968.

Moore, Clement Clarke, *A Visit from St. Nicholas*. New York: McGraw-Hill, Inc., 1968.

Morrow, Suzanne Stark, *Inatuk's Friend*. Boston: Little, Brown and Co., 1968.

Mosel, Arlene, *Tikki, Tikki, Tembo*. New York: Holt, Rinehart and Winston, 1968.

Ness, Evaline, *Sam, Bangs and Moonshine*. New York: Holt, Rinehart and Winston, 1966.

Peppé, Rodney, *Hey Diddle Diddle*. New York: Holt, Rinehart and Winston, 1971.

Perrine, Mary, *Salt Boy*. Boston: Houghton Mifflin Co., 1968.

Pflug, Betsy, *Funny Bags*. New York: Van Nostrand Reinhold Co., 1968.

Reed, Gwendolyn E., *Adam and Eve*. New York: Lothrop, Lee & Shepard Co., 1968.

Reeves, James, *Rhyming Will*. New York: McGraw-Hill Inc., 1968.

Rose, Ronald, *Ngari the Hunter*. New York: Harcourt, Brace & World, 1968.

Rounds, Glen, *Casey Jones: The Story of a Brave Engineer*. Los Angeles: Golden Gate Junior Books, 1968.

Rudolph, Marguerita, *I Am Your Misfortune*. New York: The Seabury Press, 1968.

Sacks, Raymond, *Magnets*. New York: Coward-McCann, 1967.

Schaad, Hans P., *The Rhine Pirates*. New York: Harcourt, Brace & World, 1968.

Schoenherr, John, *The Barn*. Boston: Little, Brown and Co., 1968.

Selsam, Millicent, *Maple Tree*. New York: William Morrow and Co., 1968.

Storr, Catherine, *Lucy*. Englewood Cliffs, New Jersey: Prentice-Hall, Inc., 1968.

Temko, Florence and Simon, Elaine, *Paperfolding to Begin With*. Indianapolis: The Bobbs-Merrill Co., 1968.

The Thirteen Days of Yule. New York: Crowell-Collier Press, 1968.

Tresselt, Alvin R., *Frog in the Well*. New York: Lothrop, Lee & Shepard Co., 1950.

Tresselt, Alvin R., *Thousand Lights and Fireflies*. New York: Lothrop, Lee & Shepard Co., 1965.

Udry, Janice (May), *What Mary Jo Wanted*. Chicago: Albert Whitman, 1968.

Warburg, Sandol Stoddard, *Growing Time*. Boston: Houghton Mifflin Co., 1969.

Weiss, Renée Karol, comp., *A Paper Zoo: a Collection of Animal Poems by Modern American Poets*. New York: The Macmillan Co., 1968.

Wildsmith, Brian, *Fishes*. New York: Franklin Watts, 1968.

Wondriska, William, *All the Animals were Angry*. New York: Holt, Rinehart and Winston, 1970.

Wooley, Catherine, *Andy and Mr. Cunningham*. New York: William Morrow and Co., 1969.

Wyler, Rose and Ames, Gerald, *Spooky Tricks*. New York: Harper & Row, Publishers, 1968.

York, Carol (Beach). *The Christmas Dolls: A Butterfield Square Story*. New York: Franklin Watts, 1967.

Zolotow, Charlotte (Shapiro), *My Friend John*. New York: Harper & Row, Publishers, 1968.

Appendix B
Materials for Use in the
Home and Outside[*]

BOOKS, PICTURES, RECORDS

Picture books
Story books
Nursery rhymes: Mother Goose, etc.
Books of poems for young children
Song book
Picture dictionary
Old magazines for pictures
Other pictures: animals, children, farm activities, food, etc.
Comic books for young children, selected with care
Low shelf or small bookcase for the child's books
Bulletin board for display of pictures
Recordings of songs, instrumental music, and stories
Book for keeping a record of child's activities (a diary or plain
    notebook)

COSTUME SUPPLIES

Long dresses
Coats, capes, shawls, scarves
Shoes, party slippers
Hats, caps, gloves
Ribbons, neckties
Costume jewelry: beads, rings, bracelets, pins
Pocketbook, billfold
Parasol or small umbrella
Travelling bag (small)

* Parents are to select what may seem appropriate at any given
time and make their own additions or substitutions to these suggestions.

GARDENING SUPPLIES

Flower pot with soil
Seeds: beans, corn, etc.
Shallow bowl with pebbles for bulbs, such as narcissus
Sweet potato to grow in a glass of water
Watering can or pitcher
Spade, trowel, rake, pail, for garden play outside

HOUSEHOLD EQUIPMENT

COOKING UTENSILS: saucepan, frying pan, toaster, mixing bowl, muffin tin and cookie sheet, measuring cup and measuring spoons, spoon for stirring, spatula, knives for cutting and spreading, cutting board, egg beater, clock or timer

COOKING MATERIALS: vegetables and fruit to wash and cut up; bread; butter; milk; eggs; sandwich spreads; prepared mixes for cakes, cookies, and pancakes; other standard food supplies

TABLEWARE: dishes, silverware, napkins and bibs

CLEANING SUPPLIES: dishcloth, soap, towels, sponge, cleaning cloths, pail, small broom or brush, dustpan, small carpet sweeper, dustcloth, etc.

OTHER EQUIPMENT: wastebaskets, vase for flowers, boxes, cupboard or shelves for toys, closet for clothes with rod and hooks that child can reach, furniture suitable for child to use freely

MARKING, DRAWING, AND CUTTING SUPPLIES

Paper
Crayons
Soft lead pencil
Washable paints and brush

Books for coloring, cutting out, and for connecting dots to form pictures
Blunt-end scissors
Cardboard, as in manila folders
Ruler

PETS

Canary and cage
White mouse and cage
Hamster and cage
Fish in bowl
Kitten
Puppy

PICNICS AND OUTSIDE PLAY

Sandbox
Wagon
Tricycle
Fishing rod, line, hooks (for father to supervise use of)
Boats and other toys that float
Cord or thin rope (size used for jump rope)
Slide, swing, jungle gym, see-saw at park or playground
Pail, shovel, rake, basket
Balls: soft rubberball, plastic beach ball
Peanuts in shell, marshmallows to roast, and other special picnic food

TOYS, GAMES, AND OTHER PLAY MATERIAL

TOYS: toys that move and some that make noise or musical sounds; toys that can be taken apart and put together; inexpensive cars, trucks, planes, boats; wooden train and track; blocks of several sizes and sturdy box to hold them; dolls; toy tea set; teddybear or other stuffed animal; hand and finger puppets (can be made from paper bags); balls, beanbag; modelling clay; large beads of various colors with string to thread them on; tricycle; small wagon to put things in and pull around; sandbox with pan, spoon, plastic toys, etc. for play in the sand; magnet (horseshoe) and metal objects, such as paper clips; farmyard set, if inexpensive;

GAMES: ring toss set; picture card games; Parcheesi and other games of moving counters from space to space; dominoes; hide-the-thimble (or other small object); magic box materials, such as: fork, knife, spoon, pencil, crayon, nail, apple, key, and other familiar objects (see Chapter 4); marbles; old deck of playing cards; music for rhythmic games;

OTHER: buttons (from Mother's button box); pennies and other small coins or imitation coins; piggy bank; flashlight; small bell; whistle; harmonica; nuts and bolts; wood, nails, hammer, or pegs and mallet; pebbles or seashells; boxes and cartons of various sizes; paper plates and cups; small basket for carrying objects; doll furniture and carriage; index cards, 3x5 inches (to make paper chains, etc.); cellophane tape (small roll)

Index